Common sense
about writing

Common sense about writing

THOMAS H. CAIN
McMaster University

PRENTICE-HALL, INC.   *Englewood Cliffs, N.J.*

PÉ
1429
.C3

PRENTICE-HALL INTERNATIONAL, INC., *London*
PRENTICE-HALL OF AUSTRALIA, PTY. LTD., *Sydney*
PRENTICE-HALL OF CANADA, LTD., *Toronto*
PRENTICE-HALL OF INDIA (PRIVATE) LTD., *New Delhi*
PRENTICE-HALL OF JAPAN, INC., *Tokyo*

Prentice-Hall English Literature Series
MAYNARD MACK, EDITOR

Library of Congress Catalog Card Number: 67–16381

Printed in the United States of America

Current Printing (last digit):
10 9 8 7 6 5 4 3 2 1

Acknowledgments

Hundreds of undergraduates have unwittingly contributed to this book, for most of the things in it, and indeed the general approach, come from my attempts to cope with their essays. Other undergraduates, when they learned that I was writing a book about their writing problems, cheerfully offered suggestions, written materials, and criticism. Among them I must thank especially Robert Benard, Frank Berliner, John Campbell, William Gruber, Robert Hemphill, Robert Horwitz, Christian Kaefer, Floyd Kail, Stuart Kiang, David Milch, John Wilhelm, and of course "Andrew Adamson" and "Basil Richards." At every stage, from conception of the idea to criticism of the manuscript, Maynard Mack has generously given advice and encouragement. Paul O'Connell and Barbara Conner of Prentice-Hall, Inc., have been most helpful. George and Ruth Lord, my mother-in-law Mrs. A. W. Smith, my brother-in-law James M. Smith, and his uncle James Smith all have made different and important contributions. My parents have continually given interest and understanding. And my wife Emily has helped in so many ways as to make her omnicompetence legendary.

Contents

Common sense
about writing

First read this

Imagine a shred of drama. The scene is any campus, just outside a classroom building. The time is that delicate and interesting moment just after course papers have been given back. Two juniors meet, each equipped with a paper. They are Lucky Breaks and Natural C. Plus.

NAT: So how'd you do?

LUCKY: I'm gonna slit my throat. How about you?

NAT: C+. What else? A real fine gilt-edged blue-chip C+. I mean, I've got C+ the last five papers.

LUCKY: Well, at least you know he's got you pegged. Know what I got? D. A lousy D. Paper before I get B+, paper before that C—, paper before that A—. He practically exhausts the alphabet just to get me an original grade. And then he pulls out his red pen and writes stuff all over it. The end, the margins, everywhere. Looks like it had a bloodbath or something. Hardly left room for the D.

NAT: Y'know, Lucks, I don't even read those comments any more. What I mean is, I know my grade by now. I could write the Bible and he'd just give me C+. So what difference do a lot of Mickey-Mouse comments make?

LUCKY: I know. And the worst thing is, this time I really gave it the old try. Worked all night on that lousy paper. All night. And then D. Just like that. I'd give a hundred bucks to know how his tiny mind works.

NAT: It's all luck. What I mean is, some guys he just sees the name and BAM! C+. Other guys he picks out of a hat.

LUCKY: Yeah. It's just the breaks, Nat. You just gotta get the breaks.

This cheerless little dialogue may not be entirely unfamiliar to you. In fact, you may even have taken one of the speaking parts. It is a feature of campus life. In its present revival, Nat and Lucky emit their customary cries of puzzled complaint as they get last week's papers back into their hands: Nat can't see why his grades are immobilized at C+, Lucky why his fluctuate so nervously. Of course, the handiest whipping boy is their instructor, but even Nat and Lucky sense that he is not the first cause. Somewhere behind him stands a veiled and sinister figure whom men in an earlier age would have called Fortune but who is well enough described in Lucky's colloquial rhetoric as "the breaks." The students' analysis doesn't venture beyond this superstitious intuition, however. Back they go to the library and their typewriters, preparing once more to shoot their arrows into the dark.

If you analyze Nat and Lucky's conversation, however, you will find at least three underlying assumptions:

1. The end of writing papers is grades, not good communication.
2. There is apparently no method for getting good grades.
3. So quality of writing, if grades reflect it accurately, must depend entirely on luck.

If these assumptions are true, then Nat and Lucky and a few million or so other undergraduates are in a bleak situation as far as their writing goes. It is not surprising that they feel alienated and victimized by the Great Paper-Processing System that seems devoid of meaning, rationale, or basis for hope. Unfortunately, in my experience, this is exactly how a lot of students do think about the job of writing papers: that success in it is something of a mystery and not possible to attain unless you "get the breaks."

If Nat and Lucky had pushed their analysis a bit further, they might have realized that writing need not be such an erratic process after all. To start with, both have shown some ability. Lucky does get an occasional high grade (although he finds it just as bewildering as his low grades); and Nat's permanent grade suggests that, in spite of his innocence about what makes writing good, he must have ability at least to the amount of one instructor's C+. Obviously both are capable of writing much better if they only knew how to go about it. Furthermore, if Nat and Lucky had articulated their assumptions to themselves, they might profitably have begun to question them. We can attempt to do so by reversing those assumptions.

1. The End of Writing Is Good Communication. Put in this way, the statement is as axiomatic for writing as it is for talking. Both use words to tell something. The quality of the talking or writing is not only in what is told but in how it is told. If there were such a thing as writing technique, then presumably its aim would be to help you communicate as effectively as possible. Of course, grades are important. It would be unrealistic to deny this (although I hesitate to make them the be-all and end-all that Nat and Lucky think they are). But good grades on papers are important mainly because they tell the writer he has put good ideas well.

2. Methods Do Exist to Help You Write More Effectively. The very fact that your instructors write comments on the technique of your papers suggests that the above is true. In those comments, brief as they may be, the question "What am I doing wrong?" (as well as "What am I doing right?") gets a partial answer. From them you can build up a method of improvement. It doesn't really matter that Nat and Lucky have largely given up reading comments, for if all they do is read them, then they won't help. To translate those comments into method the students will have to apply them to the next papers they write. For the goal of your instructor's criticisms is (I hope) not to make you feel bad or guilty or inferior but to help you eliminate identified faults and develop virtues opposite to those faults. Further, apart from criticisms, there are a lot of handy things that everybody should know about writing. Nat and Lucky, for instance, not only don't understand what they are doing wrong but also seem unaware of any constructive information about writing methods. Lucky seems to consider staying up all night as his main contribution to the success of his paper, but this is really not method but effort. Effort by itself is directionless and futile unless you have some technique with which to channel it.

3. You Can Control the Quality of Your Papers and Your Development as a Writer. From the discussion of technique and method in the preceding paragraph you will have guessed that I would say this. But it is not, as every writer knows, quite true. It is true most of the time, true enough to be useful. But I must also admit that there is in writing an element of luck, of the uncontrollable, of the unconscious if you like. When it comes as inspiration, a brain wave, a sudden synthesizing perception, it will be the best thing in your paper. But none of us can control it or depend on it, and in the meantime there are essays to be written. On the more pedestrian level, where most of the work of writing is done, there are techniques that will put most aspects of the writing process under your control, to the extent that you can in fact bring about a very noticeable improvement in your manner of writing from one paper to another. Because Lucky has no such technique, he can't make each paper communicate better than the last in spite of the quality of his material and the amount of his effort. Good ideas badly communicated are like a king in beggar's rags: hard to recognize.

This book is written for the Nats and Luckies of this world. Its main idea challenges their three unspoken assumptions. I hold that if the aim of writing is to communicate well, there are techniques for doing this, and by applying them you can assure and control your improvement.

Of course, I assume too that you want to learn to write better. You would be silly not to. Skill in writing is an invaluable permanent asset not only in college but later in the business and professional worlds. (How many offices with the best views are inhabited by executives complaining that their men can't write?) Further, writing skill is a highly personal asset and one not likely to be automated. In fact, the demand for it grows daily. For most people the four undergraduate years are their last crack at acquiring a solidly based, flexible, and permanent writing technique. It begins to appear that, confused by their own complaints and midnight vigils, Nat and Lucky are unwittingly missing an opportunity that won't likely come again: for four years of their lives they have to write regularly, and those papers are being scrutinized and evaluated by intelligent critical readers. Since they are now juniors it looks as if they have already thrown most of their chances away. My aim here is to help you seize your chance: first, by showing you how to turn criticism of your writing into a self-improving technique that, if you use it conscientiously, makes progress inevitable; second, by describing an orderly set of constructive techniques whereby you can take fullest advantage of each of the different operations that make up the act of writing.

Don't imagine, however, that this book contains the last word that can be said about writing technique. It is neither an encyclopedia nor a panacea. It is a short, practical guide, designed to be read quickly and referred back to easily. I have kept it small because I believe that once you know a few sensible things about technique, you should spend your time writing and not reading about writing. It contains simply some common-sense, homespun methods that, as I taught and read papers in three different universities, I found myself recalling or improvising or learning. Some of them are traditional; some come from I don't know where; some I take from students and colleagues, some from my own writing. (A student the other day, reading my description of some errors, said with insight, "You sound as if you'd fallen into most of these yourself." He was right.) I have tried to include only those techniques that, in my own experience, have helped my students or me. Those I have not found helpful I have left out. Also, I have tried to explain them in an informal manner, just as if I had the floor in a seminar or had a student trapped on the other side of my desk.

Finally, I do not believe that you can be taught to write from scratch, as if you were beginning to learn biology or Russian. You already know too much: you can speak and read English, and you even write it now and then. No matter how bad your present writing is, it is a basic accomplishment not to be ignored. For better or worse, it is what you have to start from. So my attempt here is not creative but ameliorative: to show you in the most practical way how you can develop, improve, and make forceful something you already can do.

How good writers learn: a self-improving method

CHAPTER ONE

Here are four paragraphs of expository prose. The first two come from established professional writers, the second two from skilled undergraduate writers.

In the Senate, things are different. Any Senator who can get the floor can talk as long as his wind lasts. He cannot be out of order unless he takes the most extravagant liberties. So Senate debates are often lively, often educational. They are very different from the formal pieces declaimed in the other House, often printed and sent to the voters without being spoken at all. A Senator has to persuade his colleagues, even those of his own party, or he has to intimidate them, and so the Senate has a high representation of public speakers who can discuss as well as declaim. Yet the national tradition is now for declamation. In the old days, joint debates like those between Lincoln and Douglas educated the public and kept the debaters in training. But those old days are past.

—D. W. Brogan, *The American Character*

This pointed, pungent, and concise paragraph says a great deal in a little space. It opens directly and continues with energy and forcefulness right to the end. And just beneath the prose surface we intuit the qualities of the author—straightforwardness, competence, and a sense of humor.

Here is a sharply different kind of professional writing:

Why am I so bent on conversation? For pleasure first, pure selfishness, but also because conversation is a school for thinkers and should be a school for democrats. When one finds supposedly educated people arguing heatedly over matters of fact and shying away from matters of opinion; when one sees one's hosts getting nervous at a difference of views regarding politics or the latest play; when one is formally entertained with information games or queries cut out of the paper about the number of geese in a gaggle; when the dictionary and the encyclopedia are regarded as final arbiters of judgment and not as fallible repositories of fact; when intelligent

6

youth is advised not to go against the accepted belief in any circle because it will startle, shock, and offend—it is time to recognize, first, that the temper of democratic culture is tested at every dinner table and in every living room—just as much as at school, in the pulpit, or on the platform; and second, that by this test and despite our boasted freedom of opinion, we lack men and women whose minds have learned to move easily and fearlessly in the perilous jungle of ideas.

—Jacques Barzun, *Teacher in America*

This paragraph consists mainly of one enormous, intricately structured sentence that accumulates power and suspense as it piles clause upon clause until, when Mr. Barzun finally reaches "it is time," it would be quibbling to disagree: Mr. Barzun seems unarguably right. His rhetorical ability makes us willing to accept any standards he may set up, no matter how rigorous and demanding they may be.

The following paragraph on an important Nigerian people, the Ibo, comes from an undergraduate paper written for a course in anthropology.

The aggressiveness and competitiveness of the Ibo is their most commonly marked characteristic. As Green says, "it is the go-getter that is admired. . . . A man who just sits quiet is not respected." Coleman finds Ibo "expansiveness, competitiveness, and emphasis upon acquired status" essential to the spearhead role they played in the development of a Nigerian elite and, eventually, of Nigerian nationalism. This aggressiveness stems in large part from the Ibo's long-standing poverty. Dense population and poor farming techniques long ago exhausted Iboland's thin tropical topsoil. The result was land hunger. Even before the British arrived the Ibo were apparently expanding their territory. This aggressiveness, then, has an historical background: it is generally the economically secure who can afford to play down material achievement. The story of increasingly successful British domination is generally the story of Ibo recognition that the material facts of life matter. This recognition, coupled with the aggressiveness forced on the Ibo by poverty, made them quick to adopt European ways on a large scale. An Ibo proverb sums it up: "a man must dance the dance prevalent in his time."

—John Wilhelm

This writer, a junior, packs a lot of information into a closely knit, logical paragraph. The writing is not only economical but it manages to include quotations and details to back up the more general statements. Even better, we sense behind this paragraph a lively and interested mind, intent on communicating brightly and efficiently.

Finally, here is another paragraph of notable undergraduate writing, this time from a junior's English paper on the eighteenth-century novel *Tristram Shandy*.

Tristram Shandy does not directly state his attitude toward love; rather it emerges from the way he stages and plays off one against the other the various incomplete attitudes toward love held by the members of the Shandy and Wadman households. What holds the Shandy household together, beyond mere force of habit and the desire for peace in the house, is the sentiment Uncle Toby radiates. For although all of the characters perceive reality in conflicting ways, they do manage to communicate on the level of genuine feeling. With Tristram, however, love is more: a confluence of the heart, the body, and the mind, in that order of importance. His attitude toward love is more nearly complete than that of any other character in the novel and as such is part of his radically unifying vision of reality. For just as he must "keep up that just balance betwixt wisdom and folly, without which a book would not hold together a single year," just as he encounters both Nannette and Maria, just as he sees things tragi-comically, so does he understand that the various elements of love must temper and balance each other.

—Stuart Kiang

This paragraph handles an abstract subject precisely, developing it in a set of clearly marked stages. At the end the writer sums up his main point in a climactic, accumulating sentence (a miniature parallel to Mr. Barzun's long sentence) that convincingly drives the idea home.

All four of these writers are good, but in different ways. The professionals, of course, write with more surefootedness, ease, and polish than do the undergraduates, but both undergraduates are well on the way to realizing their potential as writers. What do these four writers have in common? A partial but extremely important answer is this: *a self-critical attitude toward their writing.* All of us who want to write well learn continually from our mistakes, whether we discover them ourselves or have them pointed out to us. Even a mature professional writer who falls into infelicities of style or lapses of grammar is likely to have them pointed out in public print by critics and reviewers. A reviewer is entirely capable, given cause, of writing, "Mr. X's habit of beginning the last sentence of every paragraph with 'And' is a most tedious mannerism." Mr. X may flush as he reads this, but if he is a conscientious writer, he will make a project of deliberately looking out for and eliminating this mannerism from his work. All of us, no matter how experienced, are always in the process of catching technical errors and stylistic failures in our writing and learning how to avoid them. Of course, the less experienced writers usually have more errors to be identified and to correct than do seasoned writers, but the process of learning from one's mistakes is the same in both cases.

I do not mean to suggest that if you learn what mistakes you make and then eliminate them, you will automatically write breathtakingly. Good writing, as we shall see, does not result only from avoiding errors. But it does in part. Correcting certain errors forces you simultaneously to develop corresponding virtues. If you learn, for instance, that you use the passive voice too much and then try seriously to use it seldom, your only alternative is to use the active voice, which all by itself will give your writing energy.

While you are an undergraduate and in the paper-writing business, you inevitably receive criticism of your writing technique. Graders, instructors, and even roommates are often only too good at pointing out your faults in composition. Each bit of this criticism, when it is precise, is invaluable. But to apply those criticisms most effectively and to ensure your improvement, you need an efficient method, such as the one I will outline in this chapter. I worked it out for my own students in a sophomore seminar several years ago, after I found that three or four of them were missing their main chance to become better writers by failing to apply my precise, technical criticisms of their writing. In fact, they were descending rapidly into the gloomy underworld of Natural C. Plus and Lucky Breaks. The technique, which my students named the Errors List, amounts only to systematizing something good writers have always done, in one form or another, for their own improvement.

This technique is a basic self-correcting method, valid for everyone. If an instructor in some course in which papers are written requires you to use it, that will solve the problem of motivation. But you can make it work yourself if you really want to improve your writing skill. All you need is a little perseverance and papers that get regularly criticized. The papers need not be for English courses. History, economics, psychology— any papers will do, as long as the reader comments on the faults of your writing alone (as distinct from his criticisms of your material). If he doesn't criticize your style, however briefly, ask him to; it is your right to know what displeases a reader, and he should feel obliged to tell you. As long as you can get criticism from any responsible, intelligent source, you can manage the Errors-List technique by yourself. It is the most individual and personally relevant kind of writing instruction you could have. Using it, you become your own tutor.

Making your errors list

To make this technique work you must manage it systematically and consistently. Create your list according to the following four principles:

1. Make It Cumulative.   Write all your identified faults in a single list, even if they come from papers written in different courses. The point is not where they came from but that they have been identified as yours. No matter that there are only one or two criticisms on a single paper: get them down anyway. It will take a lot of papers to make a list that describes your personal writing problems with some tentative completeness. Above all, don't trust your memory with criticisms because you can't be bothered to jot them down. Memorize them if you can, but get them down in black and white on your Errors List first. Always make two copies of that list and keep them in different places: since this is really a valuable aid, you cannot afford to lose it.

2. Make Entries as Brief as Possible. For each error put down just enough to tell you its nature; for instance, "verb should agree with subject," not "I failed to make some of my verbs agree with their subjects," which sounds more like a confession than a technique. Sometimes you will find it handy to indicate the reason for a difficulty ("monotonous style: sentences of same length") or to remind yourself of the remedy ("passive verbs: use active"; or "padding: cut out all excess words"). The most efficient form, of course, will be the form that makes most sense to you, but keep it brief so that you can see your whole history of problems at a glance.

3. Distinguish Three Kinds of Errors. For efficiency your Errors List should have three pages, one for each category of error.

A. MAJOR ERRORS. These are difficulties that have to do with the whole paper or sections of it. They concern matters of style, organization, paragraph construction, logical argument, approach to material, and point of view. They would include errors like the following:

no logical connection between sentences
unnecessary introduction
overwriting: too many modifiers
failure to illustrate
paragraphs not developed around single points
monotonous style: sentences all begin with subjects
total organization arbitrary, lacks logic

Look for identification of major errors in your instructor's comments at the end of the paper.

B. MINOR ERRORS. These usually affect only words, phrases, or single sentences. Mistakes of grammar and punctuation account for most of them. They usually spoil the reader's impression of your literacy, not the total effect of the paper. Here are some examples:

sentence fragment
agreement of verb and subject
clichés
apologetic quotation marks
comma comes inside terminal quotation marks (,")

Your instructor will ordinarily have annotated these errors in the margins of your paper.

c. SPELLING ERRORS.   Although spelling is reasonably included under minor errors, it offers so specialized a problem for many undergraduates that a separate list makes it easier to study. Your instructor will annotate spelling errors in the margins of your paper, but you should be quick to record other useful words when you are unsure of their spelling. Correct spelling is so much a matter of visual familiarity ("it looks right") that you must be careful to put down on your list only the correct form and not the error. Record "preferred"; don't write "preferred, *not* prefered" because both will begin to look familiar.

English spelling, for historical reasons, is at present scandalously unreformed and unreasonable. Even the most literate and logical of us know words we can't spell. The excitement of the Friday afternoon spelling match in the one-room schoolhouse was that the peculiarities of English spelling made it a game of chance, even for the champion speller. But you cannot afford the spelling-match mentality when you are writing. If you are one of those persons who, in spite of seeing only the correct spelling of some words, still cannot get them right, then use the spelling section of your Errors List to remind you to look them up in the dictionary each time you use them. All of us have to do this with some words.

4. Don't Record Criticisms of the Material Itself.   Entries should refer only to technical problems of writing. It is useless to record an instructor's criticism of the actual content or argument or material of your essay. That criticism is a quarrel with what you have written, not with how you write. The sophomore who had just received my comments on his paper on Chaucer and entered on his Errors List "Wife of Bath is bourgeois, not noble" was just cluttering up the system and making it awkward to use.

Sample comment

Here is an instructor's terminal comment to a freshman paper entitled "The Effect of the First Scene of *Hamlet*." As you read it, distinguish the criticisms referring to content, argument, or opinion from those referring to technical problems of writing. Obviously you would record only the latter on your Errors List.

You have some perceptive ideas on this scene but don't present them well. I especially like your idea that the scene begins with the guards nervously looking for an enemy outside the castle while the real enemy (whoever he is) is inside. This is an insight with implications for the whole play and you should explore it further. There are some structural problems in your writing. You create a miscellaneous arbitrary effect by blurring the main point of each paragraph and failing to provide transitions and connectives between points so that I get lost and confused. By the way, I can't agree that Horatio "stands in for Hamlet" in this scene, as you assert twice without explanation. Shakespeare differentiates them very sharply throughout in spite of their own apparent attempts to merge. Notice how differently they react to the ghost here. Notice too the monotony of Paragraph 3 (read it aloud): six sentences in a row all beginning with their subjects! Vary this to break the monotony. Much too frequent use of passive verbs, too—about half of yours here. Use active whenever you can.

There are five distinct criticisms made here:

1. main point of each paragraph unclear
2. no transitions and connectives between points
3. Horatio doesn't "stand in for Hamlet" in this scene
4. monotonous sequence of sentences beginning with their subjects
5. too much passive voice: use active instead.

If you received this comment, what would you record on your Errors List? Clearly not the third, for it is a criticism of the writer's argument. Either the student is wrong, inconsistent, or unclear or perhaps the instructor is wrong; in any case the criticism expresses a disagreement about material. But the four remaining comments, all concerning flaws in writing technique, would be exactly right for entry on the major-errors page of your Errors List.

Obviously the paper on *Hamlet* was written by a beginning student who has serious and elementary writing difficulties. It sounds, in fact, as if he is much more skilled as a literary critic than as a writer. His faults have to do with organization (1), awareness of the reader's need to be led (2), and rhythm and force of style (4 and 5). No matter how grave his difficulties, however, he now knows what some of the worst of them are. The next step is to record them on his Errors List and take precautions to eliminate them from his next paper until correcting them becomes a positive habit.

Six weeks in the lives of Andy Adamson and Basil Richards

Here are the Errors Lists of two students as compiled during the first six weeks of a freshman English course in which each wrote a five-hundred-word paper per week. For my own safety I will grant them the pseudonyms Andy Adamson and Basil S. Richards. Their personalities, interests, and backgrounds are very different and so is their writing. You can see this difference at once from the major-errors page of their respective Errors Lists.* Here is Adamson's:

MAJOR ERRORS   Andrew A. Adamson

Paper

I	1. no principle to over-all organization
	2. arbitrary, meaningless paragraphing (center each around one idea)
	3. no logical sequence of thought from sentence to sentence
II	4. anticlimax in organization
	5. monotonous style: sentences of similar length (read out loud)
III	6. too much generalization: illustrate, give details
	7. too many short undeveloped paragraphs
IV	8. unnecessary introductory paragraph
V	9. monotonous style: sentences all beginning with subjects
	10. too many passive verbs! use active
VI	11. more transitions required to show logic of paragraph

*Through their joint efforts, Adamson and Richards between them compiled in six weeks a representative selection of difficulties plaguing undergraduate writing. If you don't understand why some of their errors are errors or how to correct them, turn to the Appendix. There I have described Adamson's and Richards' errors, shown how to correct and avoid them, and provided examples. Many of the errors below have been discussed at length elsewhere in this book, in which cases the Appendix will refer you to the relevant pages.

The very beginning of this list suggests some deficiency in Adamson's previous instruction in writing. Whatever the cause, he handed in his first freshman paper without any real idea of how to put it together. His initial difficulties range all the way from not knowing how to plan the paper's broad outlines, through not knowing how to compose paragraphs, to not knowing how to make sentences form a sequence of connected ideas. In this vacuum of information about writing method Adamson had assumed that the success of Paper I depended on a fortuitous blend of intuition and happenstance. In fact, he was already a kid brother to Lucky Breaks. His instructor's comments came as a surprise. They made it clear that writing is largely a technique, its quality depending not on chance but on understanding and applying common-sense principles. No doubt the instructor could have compiled a whole anthology of major errors from this first paper, but he pointed out only three as quite enough for Adamson to absorb at one time. But he also insisted that Adamson eliminate those three.

So Adamson set to work with his Errors List, determined not to commit his proven crimes again. He is a crew-cut, hard-headed, practical young man with a methodical mind in most things. When he wrote Paper II he extended, for the first time in his life, this methodical approach to his writing. You can see the results in terms of organization alone: from almost none to the rather sophisticated problem of anticlimax. In the remaining four papers he progressed toward increasingly miscellaneous problems, more concerned with style than with difficulties of elementary method.

Basil Richards is not much like Andy Adamson. He is flamboyant, talkative, often charming, sometimes outrageous, and very impulsive. He gestures with his hands when he talks and, for more vigorous punctuation, uses them in unsuccessful but persistent attempts to brush a great mane of hair out of his eyes. He has rhetorical gifts (a high verbal aptitude if you like), reads a lot, and did a good deal of not very well supervised writing in high school. Here is the major-errors section of his Errors List:

MAJOR ERRORS   B. S. Richards

Paper

I   1. copyread!
     2. inflated and repetitious: too wordy
     3. sentences all too long and complicated: qualify in *next* sentence
     4. sentences too interrupted: keep subject and verb together

II   5. overwriting: bogged down in unnecessary modifiers
     6. verbs passive: use active where possible
     7. more transitions required to keep reader oriented

III 8. verbiage, deadwood: cut! cut! cut!
     9. digressions: keep to planned organization

V   10. excessive detail: use only enough to particularize my point
     11. pretentious word-choice: use simplest *correct* word
     12. quotations not dovetailed into my text: make it fit them grammatically
     13. unjustified conclusion

VI   14. rhetorical questions overused, become mannerisms
     15. inversions of subject and verb are pompous

This list is distinguished from Adamson's by its greater length, its preoccupation with style rather than with elementary problems of organization, and the rather fine distinctions made between similar errors (e.g., 2, 5, 8, and 10). Although Richards is clearly a more experienced writer than Adamson, his progress through the first six weeks was much less steady and in fact was punctuated by two shocks. The first came when he got back Paper I with his instructor's comments and a low grade. Richards was used to praise and high grades. Moreover, his feelings were hurt that the reader not only did not applaud but was dismayed that he had written a 1,200-word paper for a 500-word assignment. He went to see his instructor at once. As a result of their long and not entirely agreeable conference he was forced to admit that he did put value on sheer length, that he was interested in how he wrote at the expense of what he wrote, and that he understood sentence length and complexity to be positive values. Richards was made to accept the humiliating fact, for him, that he had writing problems. Because he had assumed that the point of writing at all is ornamentation and not communication, he had forgotten about the reader. So Richards was put to work with his Errors List. In the next three papers he began the habit of disciplining his excesses.

His second shock came when he got back Paper IV ungraded. His instructor had refused to accept it because Richards had impatiently jettisoned the whole self-correcting system as tedious and had gone back to his old free-wheeling manner. So the faults of Paper I had recurred in IV. In fact, teaching Basil Richards was a little like bronco-busting: he had to be forced to communicate and to improve. But he had a lot of ability, which made the rough treatment his instructor gave him worthwhile. In Papers V and VI his rhetorical energy, now channeled by discipline and purpose, began to produce a truly individual and effective style. Richards never quite admitted this, however, saying only in a sour-grapes way that he was writing better now and enjoying it less.

Now look at the minor-errors sections from these two Errors Lists.

Minor Errors   A. A. Adamson

Paper

I	1. run-on sentence
	2. verb should agree with subject ("one of the examples *has*")
II	3. semicolon misused (confused with colon)
	4. "like": not a conjunction
	5. sentence fragment!
III	6. apologetic quotation marks
	7. position of comma before terminal quotation mark (should be—,")
IV	8. split infinitives (use only if no other way)
V	9. dangling participle
	10. cliché
	11. don't use exclamation points for emphasis
VI	12. instability of verb tenses
	13. avoid underlining for emphasis

MINOR ERRORS   B. S. Richards

Paper

I	1.	split infinitives
	2.	mixed metaphor
	3.	use square brackets for insertions inside quotations
	4.	too many semicolons (make separate sentences instead)
II	5.	pronoun should agree with antecedent
	6.	faulty parallelism
	7.	"to whoever has" (not "whomever")
	8.	clichés
	9.	avoid underlining (italics) for emphasis
III	10.	"as": inelegant used causally (use "because")
V	11.	"Firstly" (use "first")
	12.	"and/or" should be "or"
	13.	purple patches
VI	14.	verb should agree with nearer subject after "or"
	15.	misplaced modifiers

Adamson's grammatical mistakes here are genuine errors, some of them very serious. His run-on sentence and sentence fragment, for instance, indicate either carelessness or a basic insecurity about correct grammar. Richards also makes some grammatical mistakes but of a much more advanced kind. More of his difficulties are with small inelegancies or points of form. Yet both freshmen have some errors in common: misuse of the semicolon; a tendency to split infinitives gaily, whether for a purpose or not; attempts to use underlining or exclamation marks as an easy mechanical way of emphasis; and a loving expertise with clichés and other worn combinations of words. These problems are common to most undergraduate writing.

The third page of their Errors Lists, the spelling section, is something of a surprise:

SPELLING   A. A. Adamson

calendar	truly
potatoes	monkeys
rhythm	temperament
existence	fulfill
subtly	

SPELLING   B. S. Richards

similar	occasion
medieval	basically
all right	interfered
deferring	existence
noticeable	occurrence
forty	subtlety
receive	publicly
proceed	unmistakable
weird	embarrass
already	accumulate

Adamson has listed 9 spelling errors from 6 papers, whereas Richards has 22 from 5; that is, Richards averages 4.4 per paper as against Adamson's 1.5. Adamson, in fact, has never had much trouble with spelling, but Richards' difficulties with it date far back. His inability to spell explains why he avoided copyreading, so that the reader would confuse his misspellings with his typos. He had long ago decided that this problem, rather embarrassing to him, was beyond solution. When the Errors-List technique was forced on him, however, he found himself compelled to tackle his spelling problem honestly. Now, by the end of five papers, he has identified a healthy number of words that he cannot spell. If he cannot train himself to spell them right, he can at least know that he has to look up those words when he decides to use them and that this will save him from appearing illiterate in his finished papers. Given this approach, the problem of Basil Richards' spelling begins to look as if it might have a solution. In fact, when he graduated four years later, he was still a poor speller, but because he kept a growing list of his misspellings and consulted his dictionary regularly, no one knew it.

Use of this self-correcting system kept Adamson and Richards from turning in their junior year into cynical and frustrated Nats and Luckies, those victims of the Great Paper-Processing System. Because their instructor forced them to learn from his criticisms, they had to improve in a precise and controlled way. But given the will to learn to write, they could have done it on their own and so could Nat and Lucky if they had used their heads. So can you. The efficiency and effectiveness of the Errors-List technique stem from the fact that it applies only to you: you have to deal only with your own faults. So much is this true that after certain students' Errors Lists begin to look worn, they seem to acquire headings typical of their authors. Andy Adamson eventually labeled his "Goofs!" and Basil Richards labeled his "Index errorum." To show how these two writers developed as they used the self-correcting system throughout their four undergraduate years, I will use examples from their papers for some of the illustrations in the following chapters of this book.

Points to remember

1. Use the Errors List as a systematic technique for habitually eliminating your known errors.
2. Record errors identified by any intelligent reader and in any course.
3. Make your Errors List cumulative.
4. Make entries as brief as possible.
5. Keep lists of major errors, minor errors, and misspellings on separate pages.
6. Don't record criticisms of the content of your papers.
7. Try to memorize your errors as they come to your attention.
8. It is crucially important that before you give any paper its final form, you check it against your Errors List.

How the Greeks wrote orations

CHAPTER TWO

In a sense the Errors List is a negative technique, a way of learning what not to do. But there are also more positive techniques that show you what to do right, and some of them are very old. So brace yourself for a brief plunge into the chilly waters of history. I want just for a moment to go back to the first surviving book about writing. Aristotle, when he wrote this book, called it *Techne Rhetorike*, or *The Art of Rhetoric.* Don't panic because your Greek isn't fluent: you can see at once that the word *techne* suggests our word "technique." By *techne* Aristotle meant a regular method for doing something, in this case writing. The title itself assumes that there is an orderly, step-by-step method applicable to composition. And he organizes his little book according to the steps of that method. We might boil the method down to this: *know what distinguishable acts are involved in the process of writing and then do them one at a time.* This principle, then, goes back to the beginning of instruction about writing. It is still unavoidable if you want to write comfortably and well. If you try to write methodically, you will find yourself forced to analyze the various operations and do them one at a time, even though you don't know their names and never heard of Aristotle or any other Greek or technique or rhetoric. In fact, any modern writer who takes his writing seriously and sees it as a set of problems to be solved will unconsciously derive this old principle of analysis from his own struggle and experience. But this is the hard way. It is much easier to learn and apply the principle consciously, as writers in earlier ages were trained to do.

Writers like Shakespeare and Milton were products of a whole system of rhetorical education designed to equip them with a set of writing techniques conceived according to this old principle of separating the operations. The results are not negligible. Shakespeare's precisionist contemporary, Ben Jonson, thought that Shakespeare wrote too much from inspiration and too little according to the rules, that he "wanted art" (i.e., lacked technique). But this is Jonson's quibbling. Both writers, as scholars. have since proved, wrote with a degree of technical consciousness and observation of rhetorical precepts that is astonishing to us now. Yet the effect in Shakespeare's case suggests not bondage but freedom. Indeed, the whole point of orderly method is to free the writer to write.

The three acts of writing

There are three classical and inevitable acts that you must go through when you write any piece of expository prose. (1) To begin with, you must have something to say. You must find your material somewhere, whether from your head, from research, or from a combination of both. Classical rhetoricians would call this the process of *invention* (Latin *invenire*, "to find"). (2) When you have found all you intend to say, the next problem is to find some effective order in which to say it. The ancient writers and their successors called this process of ordering material *disposition* (*disponere*, "to arrange"). Disposition is the business of deciding on the relevance and value of your points, arranging them in groups, and ordering those groups to achieve the kind of effect you want. When you have managed invention and disposition, you know what to say and where (in the whole work) to say it. (3) It only remains to say it, to put it into the most telling prose you are capable of. The Roman rhetoricians, with the oration in mind, called this step *elocution* (*eloqui*, "to speak out or plainly"), but it is essentially what we mean by *expression*. Expression is simply "saying it" or "putting it in words." The writer who knows what he has to say and where he wants to say it has nothing to worry about except saying it well. He can really concentrate on achieving the most effective expression of his material because orderly technique has freed him to devote himself at this stage to style.

To summarize these separate acts:

1. invention—finding something to say
2. disposition—arranging it
3. expression—saying it

The order of these acts is, of course, inevitable. You can't really say something until you know what there is to say and what you want to say next as well as what you have just said. The famous quip "How do I know what I think till I hear what I say?" is meant to astound by its obvious illogicality (although it does account for some of the characteristics of cocktail conversation). It assumes perversely that expression can come before invention, that style can precede thought, that you can in fact have sentences without having meaning. As such it runs directly counter to the technique writers have traditionally assumed to be necessary and self-evident.

Order and freedom

The point of performing one single operation at a time is to make the whole process of writing easier for you. Because this technique allows you greater control over your writing, it gives you greater freedom as you write. Undergraduates all too commonly object to it as limiting rather than liberating. But the alternative to orderly process is disorderly process or, frankly, chaos. (In literature, chaos has always stood as the antithesis to the creation or making of anything.) Chaos best describes Andy Adamson's situation as he began to write his first freshman paper. He naively assumed, you will remember, that it would all fall together, that ideas would drop into place of their own accord, that, in fact, luck would be with him rather than against him. The resulting paper failed depressingly to communicate. In this case you could hardly say that innocence of technique liberated Adamson. Rather, it left him struggling to manage simultaneously all three of the basic operations—invention, disposition, and expression. Adamson did not, of course, know them or their equivalents as distinguishable operations. To him writing was simply writing. After a few hard knocks at the beginning, however, he was later cheered to discover how much easier and more efficient it was to do the operations consciously one at a time and how much more effective was the result. He began to sense his control of the medium instead of a helpless dependence on luck.

It is no doubt possible for some undergraduates to do all the operations simultaneously when the length of the paper to be written is only one or two pages. Although it is not the easiest way to write even a short paper, it can be done. But five-hundred-word papers will not be required of you forever. Regular papers of ten to thirty pages are to be expected in most colleges. Confronted with such a writing assignment you are simply asking for headache and tedium and waste of time if you decline to make the orderly performance of invention, disposition, and expression the basis of your technique.

At the University of Wisconsin, as at many universities, freshmen have to write a long "research paper" in their second semester of English. It is usually the first long paper they write. Doing invention, disposition, and expression separately and in order is essential to the assignment, although the classical rhetorical names are not applied to these operations. Invention takes the form of researching material and recording it in available and flexible form on note-cards, disposition involves arranging the cards to form an outline, and expression is the writing of the paper. Students hand in their collected note-cards, then later their outlines for criticism, before beginning to write. This is all orderly and according to the ancient and inevitable principle. But every year (at least when I was teaching there) an astonishing number of freshmen would approach me and other instructors and ask permission to hand in their outlines *after* they had written their papers. They promised that they could "make a better outline" from the finished paper. The questions of how they got the paper finished (let alone organized) and how a reader might be expected to make his way through it were apparently not broached. What these freshmen were asking for was to participate in the chaos of Andy Adamson's first paper, to leave to chance the whole delicate process of composition. Had they been granted this supposed liberty from orderly technique, their resulting bewilderment would have been too cheerless to contemplate. The prospect of a freshman continually reshuffling his several hundred note-cards to find out somehow what sentence he should write next is not only an efficiency expert's nightmare but suggests as well a new and academic theme for the Theater of the Absurd—not only absurd but masochistic. Just visualize yourself doing, say, thirty hours of this reshuffling, pencil poised, and you will be convinced that an orderly writing technique serves mainly to lessen human suffering. A freshman doing one operation at a time can efficiently proceed from note-card to note-card following the outline or disposition in which he has arranged them, knowing exactly what he has to say next and concentrating on saying it.

The strange case of Mike Harris

Much more advanced students with a history of long papers behind them sometimes boggle at the prospect of making their writing proceed according to an orderly technique. Here for instance is a Yale senior—call him Michael Harris. He is alert and opinionated, standing about in the middle of his class and underachieving. When I asked him about his use of disposition he gave the following testimony:

> I think outlining in your head is better than a formal skeleton put on paper. If you think about things for a few hours and then write whatever comes into your mind, stop when nothing more comes, smoke, think, then write again, and then piece together the whole mess it works much better. This is just personal taste, but it's the only way I can write a paper.

This man did not write badly although he was making little organized effort to develop his considerable verbal abilities. His papers were at their best original. But they had a rough-shod, ragged, hot-off-the-press quality about them—the product of disorderly method. It is clear from his statement that Harris was thinking up material, ordering it, and expressing it all simultaneously. As he describes the process it sounds on the surface casual but effective. But was it really efficient or easy? Some of his phrases betray the fact that for Mike Harris writing a paper was a slow process ("think about things for a few hours") and scarily dependent on chance ("write whatever comes into your mind," "when nothing else comes"). Moreover, he gives something away when he describes the finished paper as a "mess." Mess is as accurate an epithet for his writing technique as it is for the overflowing ashtray on his desk as he finished the last sentence. The question of the quality of his writing put aside, the real problem with Mike Harris' approach to writing is that it makes the whole process nightmarishly hard and uncontrollable. You should not be surprised to learn that he looked on each new paper assignment as a Coming Great Crisis, then ground the paper out during a hectic forty-eight-hour vigil. It is hard for me to see why "just personal taste" should make such punishing demands of a writer. Sir Philip Sidney applied his advice to himself, "Look in thy heart and write," only to the love sonnet, and even then facetiously. When Mike Harris looks in his head for invention, disposition, and expression all at once, the result is a kind of verbal juggling act, more ordeal than technique and proper only to that shadowy fatalistic limbo inhabited by Natural C. Plus and Lucky Breaks.

The three acts and the five-day week

Mike Harris' crises arose from his failure to distribute the three operations of invention, disposition, and expression over the time at his disposal. Suppose that on a Friday an instructor assigns you a five-page paper (about 1,200 words) to be handed in the following Friday. Even accepting the likelihood that you won't do much about this paper or anything else academic during at least part of the weekend, you can still fit the various operations into the rest of the week in such a way as to take greatest advantage of the distinctions between them. If we abandon Friday and Saturday, then you will have to find some time Sunday and Monday for discovering material—that is, invention. This is the most time-consuming operation because you will probably have to do some preparatory reading, perhaps some research in the library, and a good deal of thinking and synthesizing on your own before you have enough ideas and material as well as grasp of the topic to begin. On Tuesday comes the big push. Review your notes and organize them into a disposition that reflects your conception of the structure of the subject and the kind of emphasis you desire. Although it is an invaluable step, disposition does not ordinarily take much time. Then write. Make an effort to write the whole paper. You already know what to say and where to say it so that you can concentrate almost exclusively on expression, phrasing each sentence as cogently as you can. But if sentences that satisfy you don't come easily and you seem to be spending too much time over them, then do them less carefully and more quickly. More work on style can come later. The important point at this stage is simply to get a draft of the paper completed. When you have a draft, don't read it over or attempt to revise. Just put it away and forget it. You are much too close to the paper to attempt any sensible detached revision.

Take Wednesday off, as far as work on this paper goes. Keep it out of your mind, too, so that you can develop an objective attitude toward it. You will have lots of other things to do in the meantime so that by Thursday you will have almost forgotten it. This is the ideal time to revise your first draft—when you feel as distant from it as if it were someone else's work. Work especially on expression, checking every sentence for style and logic and reading each paragraph out loud to give the ear a chance to detect what the eye cannot. Type out a final draft, copyread it, sign your name, and on Friday hand it in.

To summarize this timetable:

Friday:	topic assigned
Saturday–Monday:	invention
Tuesday:	disposition and expression (first draft)
Wednesday:	forget it
Thursday:	revise, especially for style, type final version, and copyread it
Friday:	hand paper in.

Obviously the cruxes come early in the week. The earlier you can begin invention the better. If you can get it done during the

weekend, then disposition and writing the first draft need not
both be crowded into Tuesday. Or you can spread the writing
of the first draft over two days. Getting from raw material to a
first draft is the crucial step, however, and a thorough-going
disposition is the way to make it easy. Do not in any case under-
value the Wednesday fallow period and the Thursday revision:
these are critically important for the production of any com-
pactly written and effectively phrased paper. By giving you a
rest and then a second opportunity to work on your paper, they
reduce to a minimum the element of chance and put you as fully
as possible in control.

It goes without saying that not all papers are five pages long
and assigned a week in advance. But the model arrangement I
have outlined here for such a paper can be readily adapted to
fit the varying circumstances of other writing assignments. Your
knowledge of the basic principle of performing the operations
one at a time will tell you what adaptations to make to the special demands of any one paper and the way it fits into your
schedule. *Keep this rudimentary five-step sequence firmly in
mind: invention, disposition, writing (first draft), rest, revision.*
Make it the basis for adaptations suiting your own conditions.

This system is remote from Mike Harris' forty-eight-hour crisis,
which begins to look like deliberate creation of a crisis mentality.
Because he allowed no time for revision, he had to assume not
only that nothing massive would go wrong but also that there
was nothing he would wish changed if he could see his paper
with fresh eyes two days later. So he always handed in his second-
best work, rough-surfaced and without precision in the argument. But his most serious blunder consisted in his anti-tech-
nique: his contortionist's attempt to do all three basic operations
at once. The great Dr. Johnson, asked for his opinion of a
woman's preaching, replied, "Sir, a woman's preaching is like a
dog's walking on his hinder legs. It is not well done; but you
are surprised to find it done at all." The remark describes
exactly the degree of Mike Harris' success—and yours, if you
stay with him in chaos.

In the following chapters I will describe individually and more
fully the three basic operations I have here proposed.

Points to remember

1. Know what distinguishable acts are involved in the process of writing and then do them one at a time.
2. The acts are invention, disposition, and expression.
3. Orderly technique frees you to write.
4. The basic five-step sequence is invention, disposition, writing (first draft), rest, revision.

Invention: what to say

The techniques for finding material vary with the paper you are writing. At one extreme there is the brief paper or theme whose material comes completely out of your own head. Invention here is subjective. The assignment only asks that you think about a subject and then express your ideas, observations, opinions, or recollections in an essay. That withered old chestnut "What I Did on My Summer Vacation" is the classic example of the essay requiring this kind of invention. As long as you can remember what you did that summer, or can invent, you have your material. Although we may remark snidely on this tedious topic, some very sophisticated varieties of writing—from autobiography to pure creative thought in philosophy or economics —require very similar invention, largely from the writer's head. At the other extreme is the paper drawn from material quite external to the writer. Here invention is heavily objective. It depends wholly on research (whether in books or in the laboratory) and aims only at an unadulterated, undeviating report of that research. Examples of this kind of paper are the book report or report on the literature of a subject without any comment or interpretation from the writer and the straight report on an experiment in the sciences or social sciences without any effort from the writer to interpret and comment.

Obviously most undergraduate papers stand somewhere in the rather considerable range between these extremes. An ordinary history or sociology essay assignment, for instance, usually demands that you combine research in the relevant books with your own ideas and comments. Here invention is both objective and subjective. The degree to which it is effectively one or the other varies with the assignment, of course, but it is hard to exclude the writer from most predictable assignments. In the most heavily researched paper he will make himself known by his introduction, his arrangement of externally derived material, and his verbal tone. As he cites various authorities, arranges them against each other, then discriminates between them, sides with some, or synthesizes, he manifests his own way of seeing the subject. The invention of such a paper thus involves as sources both the writer's head and his research.

Undergraduate papers also vary extremely in length, and this obviously has an effect on the technique of invention. At one pole there is the freshman theme of one or two pages; at the other there is the long term paper or the senior thesis that may run to one hundred pages or more. The short theme requires only the simplest kind of technique for finding material. If it is brief enough and largely invented out of your head, a few ideas scratched down on a piece of paper and then sorted out by being numbered or by having lines connecting the related bits of material may do very well. But as soon as the problem of inventing a longer paper confronts you—even one of four or five pages, especially if it involves research or reading of any kind—you will need a smoothly working technique that can store information and your own ideas in a flexible form until you have covered the ground and are ready to arrange them in a disposition.

In spite of the variety of writing assignments, two stages are necessary for the invention of almost all kinds of papers. They are the collection of raw material and the imposition on that raw material of a thesis or focus.

Finding raw material

Searching the Topics.   If you are inventing an essay by getting material largely out of your head, your main difficulty may lie in simply getting started. How do you get ideas to offer themselves? *A classical rhetorical technique for breaking into invention is to begin by asking yourself questions about the subject.* The old rhetoricians called such a process "searching the topics."

This phrase denoted the use of handy general headings or categories ("topics") that the writer put to himself as questions about the subject.

One form of this is the seven "circumstances" taken from Cicero's treatise *On Invention* and memorized by schoolboys for centuries as a means of cracking open a resistant subject. Thomas Wilson, a sixteenth-century English rhetorician, put these circumstances into a rhyme of the "thirty days hath September" kind so that students could memorize them more readily:

> Who, what, and where, by what help and by whose,
> Why, how, and when do many things disclose.

Whereas all these questions may be appropriate only to a narrow range of subjects, such as description of a human act or of a narrative or historical event, they suggest that searching the topics may offer a basically useful and adaptable technique for finding material. Implicit in the process of searching the topics is an assumption most of us have accidentally found to be true: that we know more about many subjects than we can recall on short notice. (Examinations have a way of bringing this to mind.)

Cicero's so-called circumstances furnish only a limited list of topics to use in searching for matter. Another list of topics adaptable to a greater range of subjects might include these: *comparison, contrast, definition, division, example, contradiction, objection, qualification, implication.* Not all of these are likely to be relevant to any one subject, of course, but a few of them will often prove helpful in getting the collection of material under way. Comparison and contrast are especially useful, for you begin to see what the essence of your subject is when you see what it is like and unlike. Suppose, for instance, that you are writing about the American Revolution. What is unique about it? This question becomes less difficult if you begin to answer by searching the topic of comparison. Compare it to another revolution of which you know something, perhaps the French or the Russian Revolutions. It begins to look not much like either of them. Conflict between social classes is not so prominent an element in the American Revolution, for instance. It does not decline into a bloodbath and purges as does the

French, nor does power shift hands when the smoke clears as with the Russian. Whether you actually mention the French and Russian Revolutions in your essay on the American Revolution is not so relevant as the fact that comparing them with it gives you an insight into its uniqueness. It helps isolate the special characteristics of the subject.

In the same way you can turn other topics into questions and apply them to a subject to "search" it for material. Here are further examples of the procedure:

1. *Definition.* Do the terms need to be defined? (E.g., what does "revolution" mean? Is the American Revolution a "revolution" in a strict sense? Or is it a "War of Independence"? or a "Revolutionary War"? Is it perhaps a civil war?)

2. *Division.* Does the subject divide readily into parts? (What are the main military phases of the American Revolution? What steps led up to the firing at Lexington of the "shot heard round the world"? What were the major factions?)

3. *Example.* What illustrates the subject most clearly? (Is there a battle or other event that most typifies the Revolution or some important stage of it? What men represent it best?)

4. *Contradiction.* Is there a contradiction inherent in the subject? (Is the Revolution a war to gain political independence or an internal economic and class struggle for power? Or are both true? Is it both a challenge to and an affirmation of traditional Anglo-Saxon rights?)

5. *Objection.* Can I foresee any objection to this idea? How can I meet it? (How can I show that the Revolution is more than a war to gain political independence? What can I say to the argument that it is nothing more?)

6. *Qualification.* Would this idea work better or be more accurate or convincing if it were qualified? (Would it be more precise to say that the Revolution is primarily an internal economic and class struggle that rapidly acquires international overtones?)

7. *Implication.* What does the subject imply? Where does it lead? (What does it suggest about the nature of imperialism? about the problems of ruling colonial territories? Why do so many spokesmen for contemporary wars of "national liberation" claim the American Revolution as their historical justification? Is this often true, or is it usually propaganda?)

There could be many more. The point is not that you burden your mind with a list of specific topics or the questions they give rise to. Rather, remember that when you must find information, begin by asking yourself questions about the subject. Even when they simply point out only what you don't know, they serve to indicate where your thinking and research should begin.

Common Sense About Time.   No matter where your material originates, it is essential that you allow yourself adequate time for its invention. If you employ efficiently your knowledge of the separate operations of writing, you will find that invention properly carried out takes far more time than either disposition (which takes least) or expression. This is not to say that "just writing it up" can be a casual act. But when you have searched out adequate material for an essay, the other steps suggest themselves. Also, your time for finding material is always limited (papers tend to be due on a fixed day), and you cannot always foresee or control the amount of thinking or reading or both that it will take to find enough material. So you must begin as early as possible to provide for whatever effort a respectable amount of material may require. Though I realize that this runs counter to the near-suicidal procrastination of many undergraduates (like Mike Harris), it is true all the same. There is simply no point in knowing about the various writing operations if you don't allow yourself time to exploit the distinctions between them.

The Impromptu Essay and the Marathon Writer.   One situation in which students seldom allow enough time for invention is the impromptu essay—whether written in class or as an essay-answer on an examination. Often they mistakenly assume that an impromptu essay is a writing marathon, with the laurels going to him who fills most bluebooks. So they look once at the given subject, glance at their watches, raise their eyes to the attendant powers, lean into the traditional forward-crouch position, point their pens downward, and—suddenly—they are off! Minutes later, pages are turning, and fresh bluebooks are being called for. But what fills those bluebooks? Usually an imprecise, digressive, perhaps totally irrelevant excursus on the subject, at least for the first few pages. It is true, of course, that if you write at this pace for a while the momentum built up can eventually bring you to good, even excellent, ideas. But think of the man at the other end of the process—your reader. He can't help forming his impression of the quality of your essay from its first few pages, and if you have written them by the marathon principle, his impression will not be favorable. Even if your essay improves dramatically further on, it will still have to overcome that initial bad impression.

The moral, of course, is that you should take time to invent the impromptu essay just as you would any other. Think carefully about what you are going to say and make notes. Then indicate in what order they might appear. Then write your essay. It is perfectly safe in impromptu essays to *allow one-quarter of your time for invention*. This may seem a lot, especially when all around you people are losing their heads and turning pages, but keep cool: method pays. Think again of the reader. When he begins your essay he will see at once that it tackles the subject head on and has order. His favorable impression will be reflected in your grade. Of course, your essay will necessarily be shorter than those of the marathon writers in the class. But no reader I can imagine would be so masochistic as to prefer a feverish, rambling, disjointed essay (probably in scarcely legible handwriting) to a shorter, more efficient, better-constructed essay on the same subject. Allowing time for invention even of impromptu essays, then, is only common sense.

The Unconscious.   The most mysterious part of every act of writing (as of every human creative act) is the role of the unconscious. Technique allows us a large degree of conscious control over the writing process, and it is the aim of this book to make you aware of that technique. But some aspects of writing are beyond control, and this is especially true of invention. "I don't know what came over me," "Suddenly a thought struck me," "I've got it!" "Eureka!"—these are familiar ways of talking about inspiration or the idea that seems to come all of its own will. But to give the unconscious time to act, to produce the coup that makes brilliant sense of all your laboriously gathered material, that shows you what the subject implies, that synthesizes chaotic facts and theories in an instant of perception, or that provides just the bright idea that has been eluding you—to allow for this attractive possibility you must start invention early so as to let your unconscious mull over the subject.

One of my very best students was a Yale senior quite unlike Mike Harris: a writer of beautifully finished papers showing a highly original turn of mind. He characteristically began working on invention at the first opportunity. But often his most impressive ideas came to him when he had gone to bed for the night and was just dozing off. Then one of them might hit him; he would have to get up and make a note so that the idea would be available in the morning. This untranquil process was fruitful only because the writer started invention early. If he had begun to dig up material at a later date he would have cramped the working of his unconscious and missed the synthesizing insights that made much of his thinking exciting. You get gratis what comes from your unconscious. It is silly to miss out on what might be your best paper by arranging time so that your unconscious cannot possibly contribute.

Flexibility.   Searching the topics and giving your unconscious time to work are useful elements of invention, which in very short papers written out of your head may supply most or all the material you need. For longer papers or papers involving reading and research, however, you will also need a method of recording the relevant information as you come upon it. Such a method will be practical only insofar as it is flexible. Until you have all the material you will need and have arranged it in a disposition, you cannot be completely sure where and how and under what heading you may wish to use any one piece of it. So your system of notetaking must let you switch and manipulate your pieces of information with the greatest freedom and the least effort. The use of ordinary 4″ × 6″ (or 5″ × 8″) note-cards offers the best way of doing this (smaller cards are useless). By recording each bit of researched information or idea of your own on a note-card, you can keep all your material versatile and flexible until the last moment and can, if a better idea of arrangement strikes you, even reshuffle information during the course of writing the paper.

The note-card designed for maximum flexibility will always contain the following:

1. a heading indicating the relevance of the note to your subject;
2. accurate reference to source (author, work, page) so that when you use this information you can document it precisely in a footnote;
3. the information itself, in quotation marks if you are quoting but carefully paraphrased *in words of your own* if you are not.
4. (One more element may appear: a comment or question from you, perhaps to remind you how this information fits into your conception of the subject. Always put such a comment in brackets or initial it to distinguish it from your note.)

Andy Adamson Takes a Note. In his junior-year course in British history Andy Adamson had to write a paper on "The Meaning of the Revolution of 1688." Here is one of his note-cards:

SETTLEMENT—long-range significance

    Trevelyan, *Revolution. . .*, pp. 10–11

Argues that brief Whig-Tory unity against James II provided basis for Revolution Settlement and that Settlement thereby derives its lasting effect.

"Under it [p. 10], England has lived at peace with herself ever since. The Revolution Settlement in Church and State proved to have the quality of permanence." [p. 11]

[but needs qualification—only partially true, a nationalistic overstatement?]

Notice the heading. In it Adamson indicates to himself how he thinks this card fits into his larger subject. Obviously he foresees a section of his paper as being devoted to the Revolution Settlement. "Long-range significance" breaks that section down as precisely as Adamson can at this stage of his reading. (He might subdivide even more when he begins to organize his complete material.)

The reference to author, book, and pages is brief. Because Trevelyan's book is one of the major works on the Revolution of

1688, Adamson had to take a lot of notes from that source. It would therefore have been wasteful to copy down a full bibliographical reference for each note taken from this book. (But Adamson did make out a properly detailed bibliographical notecard for each work consulted. See below.)

In recording the information itself, Adamson is careful to distinguish between accurate quotation of Trevelyan's words and his own paraphrase, which serves here to put the quotation in something of its original context as Adamson found it. He paraphrases *completely in his own words*, however, so that later he may not *unconsciously plagiarize* by mistaking words of Trevelyan's for his own. Because his quotation happens to straddle two pages of the book, Adamson carefully distinguishes that part of it on page 10 from that on page 11. It is quite possible that he may choose as he writes to utilize only the second sentence of the quotation, which stands up strongly by itself. In that case his reference will be to page 11 alone.

Finally, Adamson puts in some qualifications of his own, distinguishing them by brackets. They assert his own attitude, not yet fully formed but potentially (if interrogatively) there, and serve to suggest what might come next in his disposition: a citation of some other study taking a less enthusiastic view of the effects of the Revolution Settlement.

You should note especially two aspects of this card. First, Adamson has made it as flexible as possible. He must because he cannot yet know for certain how he will use it. Second, he chooses his quotation with a good ear (it sounds resonantly important) and is alert to its powers of implication for his subject. Because apt quotations give the forcefulness of authority to your prose, it is usually unwise to choose for quotation a passage that is badly or weakly phrased unless your purpose is to demolish it.

Adamson also records all the facts about Trevelyan's book to enable him to make accurate references to it in footnotes and, if necessary, in a bibliography. He has included the library callnumber for convenience should he need to recheck Trevelyan later. As he recorded the bibliographical data from the title page and the date from its reverse, he cleverly noted that the book was first published in 1938 although the copy he read was a reprinting done in 1953. Thus he can caution himself that because Trevelyan wrote before World War II, his work is perhaps a little dated in its conclusions. The date also reminds him that other later studies have been able to take advantage of Trevelyan's and to be influenced by it.

Here is Adamson's note-card giving the complete bibliographical data for Trevelyan's book:

```
                 Trevelyan, George Macaulay, The

                 English Revolution. 1688–1689,

                      London: Oxford Univ. Press, 1953.

    By47C
    938T

                      (first published 1938)
```

Once he had completed his notes, Adamson had all his material before him in admirably flexible form. True, he had to find some pattern in it, arrange it in a disposition, and then write the paper. But his method of invention left him free to arrange and rearrange his material quickly and easily to achieve whatever effect he wished. Andy Adamson had first been taught how to make note-cards in high school. But it was not until his sophomore year of college, when he found himself writing five long research papers in the first term, that he realized that this method was the only practical way of handling invention. He is quite unlike the unfortunate, bemused graduate student who, through lack of foresight and innocence of method, actually took all the notes for his M.A. thesis on large yellow sheets of legal foolscap. He had recorded the relevant information book by book, page by page—not topic by topic. Entry followed entry down each interminable yellow sheet. The result, of course, was maximum inflexibility. He could not begin to organize his 175-page thesis until two less confused graduate students took rather aggressive pity on him. Armed with scissors, they cut up his great yellow pages and improvised note-cards from them. By this last-ditch expedient the raw material was reduced to a certain impromptu flexibility, arranged in order, and the thesis—for better or worse—got written.

Common Sense About Research. This point is so obvious that I would not state it here were it not for my experience of undergraduates' research habits as well as my own. Common sense suggests that your research should generally progress from more elementary to more advanced studies, and that in subjects where some of the material is difficult for you to master, you should prepare yourself by consulting less advanced sources first. But common sense is spectacularly uncommon. When I was a freshman at the University of Toronto I wrote for a course in medieval history a very odd paper on the law courts of Henry III of England. At points it seemed very informed, at others groping. Although I had discovered some remote pieces of information, my ignorance of more prominent and accessible aspects of the subject made it impossible for me to use the more advanced material intelligently. Yet I was forced to use it because it was the bulk of my material. My instructor saw from the two books of my pitiful bibliography what had gone wrong. I had first read a general account of Henry III's reign in an elementary textbook, then gone to a treatment in an augustly learned and technically detailed volume of the *Cambridge Medieval History*. My instinct to proceed from elementary to advanced was sound enough, but I had dangerously abbreviated the process. To make sense of the Cambridge historian, I should have read first some more advanced account than that in my textbook. Because in my freshman stupor I didn't think to do this, I wrote the paper profoundly puzzled about Henry III and his courts, desperately putting down bewildering information. The result was truly pedantic: it had the learned-idiot effect.

You should be aware of three clues to the intelligent control of the progress of any research, although their relevance depends on the nature of the source material:

1. Proceed from the most detailed basic treatment that you can understand to more advanced treatment.
2. When an advanced study goes beyond your depth, find one of intermediate difficulty and use it to prepare yourself for the advanced.

3. But don't spend too much time on very elementary material and unnecessary background, or you may never get the paper written at all. Writers who begin reading very far away from their subject and hope to build up a complete background for it usually are not being practical about time. Often they simply capitulate or else at the last frantic moment do only minimal research and write papers thin in content.

Finding an argument or focus

As the last stage of invention, you must assume an attitude toward your subject that will coordinate it and give it a single direction. This attitude may take the form of either an argument or a focus. By *argument* I mean simply a defensible position regarding the subject (i.e., the form taken by most debating resolutions). "Dutch elm disease" is a subject, but "Dutch elm disease can be controlled" is an argument, implying automatically that its opposite is untrue. By *focus* I mean any nonargumentative way of seeing unity in the subject. Focus usually reflects a discernible principle inherent in your raw material. "How Dutch Elm Disease Spreads," "The Effect on Rural Landscapes of Dutch Elm Disease," "Urban Spraying Programs for Controlling Dutch Elm Disease"—these hypothetical titles bring three unifying focuses to bear on the subject. They are not argumentative but are instead simply approaches to the subject "Dutch elm disease" that allow you to begin ordering your collected raw material.

This stage of invention will be irrelevant if the topic set for the paper has forced you to collect your material with the intention of taking a predetermined position. Essay assignments that begin "Show that," "Argue," "Defend," "Prove," "Criticize," or "Reply to" obviously have argument built into them. Topics like "The Social Effects of Heroin" or "The Administration of the Federal Reserve Bank" obviously have a controlling focus inherent in them: the variety of the effects or the shape of the administration will automatically structure your collection of material. In such topics, argument or focus has been externally imposed, and consequently this second stage of invention is not relevant.

But in topics where only a subject without imposed argument

or focus has been assigned, it will be necessary for you to find one. You may be able to decide on an argument or focus early in your collection of material or even before you begin. But more often you will have to collect some or most of your material before you know what argument or focus is possible.

Suppose you have to write an English paper, for instance, on the first scene of *Hamlet*. You will have to read the scene as well as the rest of the play, making notes on the material—from the text and from your head—that occurs to you as being probably useful. When you have done that you may find as you look over your material that it suggests an argument, perhaps one something like this: "the first scene lays bare an initial form of the central problem of the play and hence is indispensable." Thus you will have construed your topic as an argument for the relevance of the scene. Now you are ready to sort out your material to marshal support for this argument. You will then know whether it is necessary for you to collect more material.

On the other hand, the material you have gathered on the subject may not suggest an argument to you at all. Instead it may suggest simply a special way of regarding the scene or a recurrent theme that develops in it and gives it structure or significance. A recurring idea in your raw material may bring this to your attention. It might be something like this: "three kinds of illusion characterize the scene." Or perhaps this: "it is organized by a progression from looking outward to looking inward." There are as many possibilities as there are ways of reading this scene. But until you have come upon one of them—either as argument or as focus—you are not ready to sort out your material or begin disposition.

Finding when necessary an argument or focus is legitimately an aspect of invention because, until you have done it, you really don't know the limits of your material, what is relevant in it, and whether you need to look for more. When found, it provides the principle for selecting and sorting your material and shows you what to look for if you need more. You can usefully make your argument or focus take the form of a single sentence; for example, "By foreshadowing the rest of *Hamlet* the first scene becomes indispensable"; or "Three varieties of illusion characterize the first scene of *Hamlet.*" Such a sentence epitomizes the structure of the whole paper. It need not necessarily appear in your finished essay, but having it in front of you is an invaluable technique in arranging your material: by summing up your attitude toward your material it furnishes the clue to disposition.

Points to remember

1. Search the topics. Ask yourself questions about the subject.
2. Allow adequate time for invention.
3. In impromptu essays, allow one-quarter of your time for invention.
4. Give your unconscious time to work.
5. Record material in the most flexible form on 4″ × 6″ note-cards.
6. Proceed in your research from basic to more advanced material.
7. Look for the principle inherent in your raw material—whether argument or focus—and use it to help limit and select your final material.

Disposition: where to say it

CHAPTER FOUR

You now have something to say. Your real problems are two: (1) to say it so that your reader understands it and, if you can make him, accepts it; and (2) to say it as efficiently as you can so that the process of writing exacts from you as little blood, sweat, and tears as possible (it will always exact some). At this stage, then, you have responsibilities to your reader and to yourself. To manage them you need the techniques of disposition. This means order. It means a firm organization of material. But it is also just at this point that the undergraduate writer, like Mike Harris, tends to rebel. As he does so he puts himself in danger of losing control over his material and consequently abdicating his responsibility to his reader and to himself. Until the writer has put a workable order on his material, he cannot expect to establish the reader's confidence in that material. Nothing scares a reader away so quickly as a suspicion that the text he reads has no design and that the blind are leading the blind through an intellectual No Man's Land. The design may not be at once apparent, of course. But the reader needs to sense it, for reading is an act of faith in the writer's good intentions. We are all too busy to read the aimless and the uncontrolled and are angry if we find we must. As soon as the reader says "This doesn't seem to be going anywhere," you have flunked disposition. Further, until you have put a workable order on your material you can't be free to write.

Common sense about outlines

If ordered material is essential, why do so many undergraduate writers balk at ordering it? The reason, I think, is that "outline" is a dirty word. To most people it connotes the sterile and mechanical, something that perhaps looks like this:

I. _____
  A. _____
    1. _____
      a. _____
      b. _____
    2. _____
      a. _____
      b. _____
  B. _____
    1. _____
      a. _____
      b. _____
    2. _____
      a. _____
      b. _____

II. . . . and so forth.

To me, this is a blueprint for the Tower of Babel. Indeed, lots of students have faked this kind of outline when they had to hand it in in some composition course. They faked it because they simply couldn't write from such an elaborately preplanned and predigested scheme of material. As a result they now refuse altogether to outline. They find themselves in Mike Harris' position, in which smoking and hoping substitute for order

Obviously we are caught here between two unacceptable extremes. For most people the Tower-of-Babel outline is much too restrictive, affording too little freedom. On the other hand, Mike Harris' laissez-faire approach is inefficient: it mistakes license for liberty and leaves him free only to stare at the corner of his room (for license restricts more subtly). The way out of this dilemma is some workable compromise about disposition that orders your material sufficiently to allow you to concentrate on style and at the same time allows enough freedom to let your imagination work creatively. Just as in invention note-cards are useful only insofar as they are flexible, so in disposition. *You should make your method of disposition flexible by adjusting two factors to each other: your own writing temperament and the nature of the material.*

The Tower-of-Babel Outline.   In spite of the unkind things I have just said about the Tower-of-Babel outline, it does work for a few people handling certain highly researched subjects. If you find that that kind of elaborately detailed outline works for you (or works for you in certain kinds of essays), then go ahead and use it. There is nothing inherently wrong with it as long as you don't find it stultifying and restrictive. In making such an outline you should beware of the artificial, however: it is all too tempting to put down headings and subheadings that add more stories to the Tower but don't represent any real information; that is, avoid the mere appearance of completeness. Put down only those headings that represent material you have on hand. Otherwise, your elaborate formal outline, deceptively complete on paper, will undeceive you sharply when you begin to write and find that some of your subheadings are virtual blanks. Above all, never allow the formal outline to become an end in itself. It is instrumental, worth doing only insofar as you find it useful in freeing you to write. If you find it restrictive, by all means use a more flexible technique of disposition.

The Scratch Outline. For very short papers the skimpiest outline will usually serve. Scratch down your main points, putting under each the details that go with it, and then arrange those points according to your argument or focus as derived from invention. Number the main points to indicate the order in which you want to treat them and then go ahead and write. This kind of disposition is really appropriate only to papers in which you can keep all the material in front of you at once or on one or two pages. In examinations and impromptu class essays, it is usually the only available technique of disposition.

A More Flexible Technique for Disposition. Most college papers are complex enough to require a technique of organization fuller than the scratch outline, however. What most of us need is a working compromise between the Tower-of-Babel outline and none at all. The following technique seems to me reasonably flexible. It gives me enough sense of direction to inspire confidence and to let me concentrate on style and clarity, and at the same time allows me freedom to incorporate the unpremeditated ideas that develop as I write. Most of my colleagues as well as most undergraduates whose writing is individual and forceful use some sort of variation on this system. It contains three steps, but these could be revised to suit your own inclinations and the specific demands made by your material.

1. With your argument or focus firmly in mind, sort your cards into *groups or blocks of material* according to subject.
2. Decide on the *order* of the separate groups of material as dictated by the argument or focus.
3. Take your first block of material, sort out the cards in the order you want, and then do *a little scratch outline* for it, including any new ideas that may come to you. Then write. Do the same for each succeeding block as you come to it.

The strategy behind this kind of outline is division of the material, however proliferated, into small units that can be handled separately by scratch outlines. In this way you can concentrate on one segment of your material at a time, rethink it while you write, add to it as ideas come to you, and keep all the material relevant to it in front of you at once. This technique is flexible enough for nearly all undergraduate papers and writing temperaments. It is the method I am using as I write this book.

All three steps require you to perform acts of ordering—in (1) the cards themselves, in (2) the blocks of material themselves, and in (3) the material inside any one block. The process of ordering is much greater in scope in Step 2 than in Step 3, of course, but it is essentially the same. As a guideline to the process of ordering, *first ask yourself what point you think most important.* (This applies both to the order of the blocks and to the order inside the blocks—that is, to Step 2 and Step 3.) Once you have decided which point is most important, then *ask yourself where it should go to be most effective.* A much circulated bit of dogma on this subject insists that the most important point should come at the end because the end is always the most emphatic position. (People who give this advice apply it promiscuously to whole papers, individual blocks of material, and paragraphs.) It seems nonsense to me. Take the frequent situation, for instance, where your most important point is also fundamental to the reader's understanding of all the rest of your material. Obviously that point has to come at the beginning—its only effective, useful, in fact necessary position. If it were withheld until the end, everything before the end would be incomprehensible. Common sense suggests that you should place the key point wherever you think it will usefully serve your purposes—beginning, end, or anywhere in between. In some very sophisticated writing the author makes us aware of the governing idea without fixing its position at all but by insinuating it repeatedly throughout the various blocks of material so that it becomes clear by a kind of osmosis. This process is too tricky for any but the most gifted and skilled undergraduate writer, however. The most practical technique for you is simply to ask the question "Where will the most important point go?" When you have decided that, then the order of the other points will likely suggest itself. If you decide that the major point would be ineffective at the end, reserve some other point of weight for that position, so that your paper does not seem to end with a whimper. (Deliberate and obviously calculated attempts to end with a bang are often worse, however. Their phoniness can be unmistakable.)

The outline as route-marking

The outline is more than a necessary aid to the writer: it also serves to orient the reader. In the finished essay, then, something of the outline should be discernible. The writer may force it inescapably on the reader's attention ("There are three major late-Victorian styles. The first is . . .") or he may use his art partially to conceal it while still keeping the reader oriented ("Among the late-Victorian styles the neo-Gothic . . ."). Much contemporary prose makes its basic structure forcefully apparent without embarrassment and is the better for doing so. It is thus analogous to certain functional types of modern architecture that make the structural elements serve also as part of the finished effect. Andy Adamson habitually writes this way. Basil Richards, as you might guess, sometimes prefers to conceal his basic structure. He thinks Adamson's method inelegant and artless, rather like visible underwear. Nevertheless, in very difficult material where he must struggle to make the reader understand, Richards also makes the outline vigorously apparent. The difference is simply one of taste. *The main point is that the outline should be enough in evidence to ensure the reader's orientation.* He must always know where he is, why he is reading what he is reading, and where he is to be taken. You may not always tell him frankly that there are, say, three main ideas in your essay, but you will at least have to make him aware of each of the three as he comes to it.

I prefer Adamson's open and obvious method of pointing out the structure of his papers. It has the advantage of making the divisions and progress of the paper so apparent that the reader has no chance of getting lost. But this method should be tempered with a little art so that the writer does not appear obsessed with the structure of his paper. The outline is not the paper itself. If it is too much in evidence, the paper will seem skeletonized—all comb and no honey. Further, if the *enumeration of points* or divisions or stages of an argument is useful, say "first," "second," and so on, not "firstly," "secondly." But if enumeration goes beyond "fifth" or "sixth," find some other method, like simple numbering in Arabic, like (1), (2). Obviously "eleventh" or "seventeenth" sounds silly and baffles rather than clarifies.

There is also a hazard in Basil Richards' more restrained and artful method of indicating structure without actually saying in words what that structure is. Whereas Adamson runs the risk of drawing too much attention to the structure, Richards at the other extreme may forfeit his reader's sense of direction by not offering enough signposts. Once you lose your reader, everything you say loses its validity: you seem to have taken back the compass and left him in the elephant grass.

Not only undergraduates but more advanced writers are capable of abandoning their readers. As an examiner of a Yale Ph.D. dissertation I was confused to find that one thirty-page section toward the end seemed irrelevant. I could follow its argument but had no idea how I had been brought to it and why I was expected to understand it. Rereading did not help. The problem was simply that the writer had neglected as he began that section to indicate how it related to what he had already said and to his larger argument. He lost me because he forgot about me. So that large chunk of his argument, though internally coherent, remained a dead loss. This incident suggests that it is safer to favor Andy Adamson's extreme: you may guide your reader a bit too forcefully, but at least you will not lose him and thus fail to communicate.

Two special problems in disposition

Comparison and Contrast. Although many college papers demand this form, most undergraduates fail to organize such a paper attractively. Suppose you are comparing and contrasting A and B. A badly organized paper will have gone wrong in one of two ways: (1) *The do-it-yourself comparison.* You devote a long section to A, a similar section to B, then attempt to pull them together in a third section. Although this method appears to work in very short papers, it always entails waste: the third section inevitably must repeat much of what was said in the other two. Such an outline abstracts to this:

1. A
2. B
3. A and B

Though deceptively simple to organize, such uneconomical comparisons annoy the reader who must read much of the same information twice. Worse, the third section is often very slight ("So you see how B compares to A"). The reader must then do for himself the real work of comparison, using the information given him about A and B simply as raw material.

(2) *The seesaw comparison.* Like many people I was taught in school to avoid the do-it-yourself comparison by making each point of comparison the unit of organization and applying each to A and B. The result would reduce to this:

1. A and B
2. A and B
3. A and B, etc.

This method approaches the business of comparison with a straight-arrow seriousness. It honestly intends to do the job for the reader. The difficulty lies in its rigidity. From beginning to end the reader feels himself jounced regularly back and forth from A to B in a tediously predictable rhythm, like being on a seesaw or watching the pendulum motion of a grandfather clock. Such grimly organized comparisons are grimly read.

THE MIXED METHOD. Once again, salvation from the unsatisfactory extremes lies somewhere in the middle. The do-it-yourself outline leaves most of the work to the reader, the seesaw outline does too much too rigidly. The solution is to have a little of the best of both worlds by mixing the methods so as to cancel their respective disadvantages. First, decide what your bias is, which of *A* or *B* you wish to favor or put forward. There is not much point in doing a comparison for its own sake: we are usually particularly interested in either *A* or *B*. Suppose your real interest is in *A*. Then the best strategy would be to use comparison as a method of especially defining *A* by seeing it in silhouette against *B*. This suggests a method of organization somewhat like the following:

1. Briefly indicate your main interest in *A*.
2. Then concentrate on *B*. (This gives you perspective from which to see *A*.)
3. Now concentrate on *A*, exploiting the perspective achieved by Step 2. Thus, you establish a way of seeing *A* from the vantage point of *B*, as well as of seeing them together. Follow with discussion of distinctive areas of comparison.
4. (specific point) Focus on *A* but call in *B* to establish the special quality of *A*.
5., 6., 7., etc. Other specific areas of comparison.
8. You may wish to bring *A* and *B* together at a level of generalization. Or you may concentrate exclusively on *A*—what has been learned about it from the foregoing exposure to *B* and what the implications are.

This is only a rough paradigm of a mixed method for organizing comparison. You will have to adapt it to specific topics. It is an especially valuable method for the most useful kinds of comparison: where *A* and *B* initially seem similar but prove to have subtle and interesting differences or where *A* and *B* seem superficially unlike but prove to have much in common.

In an anthropology course, for instance, Andy Adamson wrote a paper comparing two primitive societies, the Ashanti of West Africa and the Blackfoot of the American plains. When he had collected his material he found that although the Ashanti and the Blackfoot seemed similar at first, they soon proved to be significantly unlike, with the Ashanti far more interesting. So Adamson organized his comparison by the mixed method outlined above, focusing on the Ashanti and using the Blackfoot as a means of gaining perspective. I have reduced this paper to a summary to make the use of the mixed-method structure more apparent. Note that *A* above equals "Ashanti" here, *B* equals "Blackfoot," and that the numbers of the steps are the same.

1. The Ashanti of West Africa formed a new and powerful society at the beginning of the eighteenth century. It depended on Europeans for its success, because the Ashanti needed guns and a slave market for their captives taken in war. By 1900, this people had been ruined by the death of the slave trade and the ambitions of the British Empire. Nevertheless, the Ashanti have stayed powerful enough to make their influence felt in Ghana, one of the most important of the emergent African nations.

2. To see another primitive people in a similar situation we may turn to the Blackfoot Indians. The Blackfoot were once small-scale hunters who lived in the Saskatchewan River valley and grew a little tobacco. After 1730, they obtained indirectly both guns and horses from Europeans, migrated, and became powerful Plains tribes, unbeatable in war. But, by 1870, the Blackfoot had been broken by the slaughter of the buffalo herds and the westward drive of the homesteaders. Today, unlike the Ashanti, the Blackfoot are a reduced, pathetic, disorganized people.

3. Of these two primitive peoples who were both raised and ruined by expanding European civilization, only the Ashanti have remained intact and vigorous. Why? Is it only because the British expansion into their territory was reluctant (undertaken only because the Ashanti made a nuisance of themselves and thwarted British ambitions on the coast), whereas in the American west the expansion was forceful and aggressive, expressing a fairly well-articulated program of genocide? Or is it because of differences in the Ashanti and Blackfoot societies? I will discuss factors in Ashanti society which made it better able to bear European pressure.

4. *Government.* Like many African peoples, the Ashanti were (and still are) good at organizing social relations. Used village organization as basic unit, organizing whole nation on village pattern. Land inherited through a lineage system descended through women, but village authority exercised by men. System for choosing leader. These factors make for stable society.

The Blackfoot were nomadic and loosely tribal, however. No rigid family organization. Loose leadership. But warriors grouped into a complicated system of clubs.

5. *Religion.* Symbolic significance of the stool owned by each Ashanti man, related to the heaven-sent golden stool of the king which contained the soul of the Ashanti, so sacred the king could only lean his arm on it. Golden stool a central symbol for the whole people, still powerful. Stools of ancestors venerated as signs of the historical unity of the race. Hierarchy of priests and medicine men. Ashanti religion was a cohesive and uniting force.

Blackfoot religion was not a national force in this sense. Emphasis instead upon private religious experience with medicine bundles (pebbles, feathers, etc.) to remember it by. These were held very sacred. Main public and tribal religious event was annual sun-dance.

6. *Economics.* Ashanti economy based on agriculture and trade. One of the main exports were slaves captured in war. Warlike qualities of Ashanti due largely to economic ambitions. Traded in gold. Practiced crafts and taught them to children.

Blackfoot economy concentrated on killing buffalo and stealing. Scarcely an economy at all.

7. *War and peace.* Ashanti had great respect for law and order. Peace an ideal. War as a means to accomplish purposes.

Blackfoot treated war more as a game and as an end in itself. Its goal was to prove the individual man's courage. Order of honors in war very important, including recognition for stealing guns, bows, horses, etc. Bravery far more important than survival.

8. The Ashanti remain intact as a people (in the mid-1950s they asked for political autonomy). The reason lies in the nature of their society. This socially interwoven and purposive people was better able to stand up to European incursion than the Blackfoot and was able to readjust itself radically twice within two centuries. But peoples like the Ashanti, with their strong sense of societal identity, pose a continuing threat to the large and often unstable countries that seek to contain them politically.

Essays Explaining Texts.   By this I mean any writing assignment that requires you to expound the meaning, system, development, or technique of a designated text. It could be a history paper explaining and commenting on the significance of a constitutional document, a philosophy essay expounding a section from Plato or Heidegger, or an English essay of literary criticism, say a discussion of a Yeats poem or a Faulkner short story.*

---

*The special problems involved in finding and ordering material for student essays in literary criticism are dealt with efficiently and attractively by Edgar V. Roberts, *Writing Themes About Literature* (Englewood Cliffs, N.J.: Prentice-Hall, Inc., 1964).

In short, you have a text in front of you and must discuss it. I have only one point to make about this, and it is based on a lot of experience: confronted with the problem of discussing a text, undergraduates tend to organize their discussion in a step-by-step orderly progress through that text. Thus the text itself provides the order for their essay expounding it. This sounds efficient and is an easy method of organization. But it results in an essay that stands as a pale shadow of the original text instead of an independent essay on it. If you let A stand here for "Next he says. . ." and B for "This means . . ." or My reaction to this is . . ." then you get a disposition like this:

1. A and B
2. A and B
3. A and B, etc.

It is exactly that of the seesaw comparison and has the same predictable and monotonous "He says"/"I say" rigidity. To paraphrase or summarize a text and at the same time comment on it yourself is properly a job only for the very skilled writer. For a less skilled writer, however, it is much safer to avoid paraphrase and summary as the structure of your essay. Instead, *organize it by concepts, not paraphrase.* Make your own ideas about the text the basis of your organization and use relevant pieces of that text as illustration and detailed proof. This makes your organization exactly like that of any ordinary essay structured by main points or ideas (the blocks or groups of material in your outline), with the one difference that a single poem or document is its subject and partial source. But the main source is you—your reading of and reaction to that document. Such organization makes this honestly clear.

Here are two short papers, both written by freshmen of similar ability, on Robert Frost's familiar poem "Mending Wall."* The first sticks doggedly to the order of the poem for its organization,

*From *Complete Poems of Robert Frost.* Copyright 1930, 1939 by Holt, Rinehart and Winston, Inc. Copyright © 1958 by Robert Frost. Copyright © 1967 by Lesley Frost Ballantine. Reprinted by permission of Holt, Rinehart and Winston, Inc., and Laurence Pollinger, Ltd.

forcing the writer to use again and again a "then Frost says"/ "this means" formula.

ROBERT FROST'S "MENDING WALL"

Frost begins "Mending Wall" with the line, "Something there is that doesn't love a wall." This line, repeated later, is associated with the attitude of the poet speaking here and is definitely not shared by his neighbor, the other character in the poem.

Next, Frost tries to identify the "something" that causes stone walls to fall down during winter. The gaps in the wall, he says, are not like the "work of hunters" who sometimes tear holes in walls to let their dogs get at a rabbit. By this indirect or negative definition Frost means that the agency that brings walls down can't really be explained except as an elusive force or principle in nature, a mysterious "something." But he can get no closer to defining it than this.

Then Frost explains how every spring he and his neighbor meet to repair the wall separating their properties. He describes the operation as a juggling or balancing act with the stones likely to fall down again at any minute. "We have to use a spell to make them balance," he says. As he thinks about it, the more impractical the annual wall-mending appears, "just another kind of outdoor game."

At this point Frost begins to associate himself clearly with the "something"—the force that wants the wall down. He does this by turning the "outdoor game" of balancing stones into a game of words with his neighbor. This little game occupies the second half of the poem.

The game begins with the poet's questioning for the first time the usefulness of the wall and his neighbor's replying with a proverb, "Good fences make good neighbors." This unoriginal statement suggests that the neighbor is unwilling to think for himself; he retreats intellectually behind a bit of country platitude just as physically he stands entrenched behind an inherited tumble-down wall.

At this point Frost the narrator attempts to draw his neighbor out of this entrenchment by shifting the grounds of argument. Instead of questioning the wall's usefulness, he moves on to question the applicability of the "Good fences" proverb. "Does it still fit?" he says (if I may paraphrase his speech). "Are walls always good?" And then he reasserts his key line, "Something there is that doesn't love a wall," adding, as if he felt he must confront his neighbor's forcefulness with some of his own, "That wants it down." Frost still won't go farther in identifying the "something," however, or in teasing his neighbor to ask questions and think for himself. He lets the game stand here.

This brings us to the closing of the poem, an impasse in which Frost pictures his neighbor as "an old-stone savage armed"—that is, a primitive, paleolithic man. This simile suggests that, through refusing to use his mind, the neighbor is less than fully human. "He will not go behind his father's saying," says Frost next, seeming to mean that the neighbor is also not mature; intellectually he still lives in his father's shadow and, worse, likes it. This, however, is the narrator's own private view. He has made no impression on the neighbor who, at the very end of the poem, repeats to himself with relish, "Good fences make good neighbors." In other words, he is more entrenched than ever. Frost's attempts to make him think have backfired and the wall-hating "something" will go on being frustrated by wall-mending every spring.

The second writer has worked out a disposition of his own to express three of his ideas about "Mending Wall": that (1) the poem presents a debate in which (2) neither side holds a tenable position, (3) thus forcing the reader to step back and see the whole poem as a "game."

"ONE ON A SIDE"

In Robert Frost's poem "Mending Wall" the narrator and his neighbor meet to repair winter damage to the ancient stone wall separating their New England farms. As he works, the narrator begins to question the usefulness of this annual ritual. His attitude basically is that an unnecessary wall contradicts some force in nature: "Something there is that doesn't love a wall, / That wants it down." His more traditionally minded neighbor counters this blasphemy with a bit of country folk-wisdom, "Good fences make good neighbors." "Mending Wall," then, contains a debate. As in any debate, the audience expects to take sides. But what side to take here is another question. Frost's strategy in the poem is to mislead us into agreeing with the narrator only, then to hint that any partisan approach to the poem is inadequate.

It is natural, of course, to see a narrative through the narrator's eyes. At first his position here sounds liberating and attractive. He would prefer to leave the "gaps two can pass abreast," while his neighbor wants to perpetuate a restrictive situation in which "We keep the wall between us as we go." Obviously, they hold two opposed views of what makes "good neighbors." The narrator's is fraternal or communal, his neighbor's legalistic and traditional.

While it is tempting to dismiss the neighbor's uncritically conservative position as altogether too rigid, he is too good-humored to be quite the defensive "old-stone savage armed" that the narrator imagines. But the narrator's own more attractive position will not do either. He undermines it fatally early in the poem when he admits that the process of wall-mending begins each year at his initiative ("I let my neighbor know beyond the hill"). Later, he tempts his neighbor to name the force that wants the wall down, although he himself can't identify it precisely:

> I could say 'Elves' to him,
> But it's not elves exactly, and I'd rather
> He said it for himself.

Finally, the narrator's attempt to make his neighbor think makes him instead more content than ever with the formula "Good fences make good neighbors." So the narrator's efforts are riddled with ironies.

Given this dilemma, what point of view is the reader to take? We have to look beyond the debaters, I think, and see the whole action of mending the wall as "just another kind of outdoor game,/One on a side." The physical action is a "game" in the sense that the narrator and neighbor both compete and cooperate in the tricky business of getting stones back into equilibrium: "We have to use a spell to make them balance." But there is also a similar problem in the psychological game or debate. For in this game the narrator must play his liberating gesture and the neighbor his restraining gesture in such a way as to "make them balance" as well as the stones. Neither is satisfactory or adequate in itself, just as neither neighbor could mend the wall by himself and still have a "game." A diagram of this "balance" appears in the construction of the poem itself, where the two key lines alternate in a parrying movement, with one also beginning and the other ending the poem. This interlocking pattern of "balance" suggests that "Mending Wall" itself is more important than its narrator, who begins to feel the limits of his own views when he says of his neighbor, "He walks in darkness *as it seems to me.*" Frost the narrator of the poem is not identical with Frost the poet, then. For the poet here forces the reader to take a larger view than does either of the characters and to play for himself the "game" of balancing contrary positions "one on a side." It is easy to see how this strong and subtle poem might have political and social implications. For it invites us to see things from a point of view where radical and conservative, internationalist and isolationist, innovator and traditionalist oppose and complement each other in a necessary tension.

Notice how much further into the subject the second writer gets, simply because of his own more practical disposition. The first writer, who has some good ideas too, can't take them far enough because his rigid Procrustean disposition forces him to account somehow for every step of the poem. What he can't quote or paraphrase, he must summarize. Even when he does this skimpily, little room remains for his own ideas, and their order has already been dictated. Like the snake-charmer's cobra, he seems hypnotized by what he sees in front of him. By using an independent disposition, however, the writer of the second paper has freed himself to write about "Mending Wall" as he sees it.

Getting started: the perfectionist's block

Now invention and disposition are complete—you have your material and have worked out an outline. But as everyone knows, being technically ready to write and being psychologically ready do not necessarily go together. More and more undergraduates (and graduate students too) block when they try to get the first few sentences down on paper. Increasingly, it seems, students appear in my office to ask for extensions or to excuse late papers. "Look, I've done the work but I just can't get started writing." This would all be very tedious but for one odd fact: the students who can't get started are often among the very best in a course. Further, they are commonly juniors and seniors of perfectionist tendencies.

I am not competent to discuss the emotional basis of this block, but I can record what I have observed. Writers' perfectionism seems to manifest a kind of pride laced with despair. The student wants to write with the excellence he feels is his, but unacknowledged doubt about his real ability undercuts his confidence and keeps him from making a start. As long as he doesn't put a paragraph on paper, his confidence in his ability to write breathtakingly remains unchallenged. Indeed, an insecure writer sometimes finds the material and the outline of an unwritten paper comfortingly tentative. He knows they can be cheerfully shifted and changed until the last moment when words actually go down as sentences and paragraphs. After that he sees himself (unreasonably) as committed permanently to his material. (Students who revise as they write are especially vulnerable to his kind of block.) Sometimes the dilemma becomes chronic so that the student can't write any papers and must leave school or go under the care of a psychiatrist. More often when the now-or-never crisis comes the writer manages at last to break through, grinds out a few agonized sentences, and then begins to write in near panic but also with an ease that surprises him. As he writes, he curses himself for not getting started earlier so that he could really polish his paper. Mike Harris had a variety of this problem and Basil Richards tangled with it in his junior year.

Apparently the real block lies not in writing itself but in getting the first few sentences down on paper. Then the barrier against communication is broken, the writer has sacrificed his perfectionism on the altar of reality, and things begin to move. The problem of blocks lies somewhere in the realm of the uncontrollable. But there are a few very homespun tricks that may help you get down those first few sentences.

1. *Don't think about yourself writing.* Concentrate instead on your subject.

2. *Don't begin at the beginning,* especially if there is to be an introduction (introductions are a notorious cause of blocks and create special problems discussed in Chapter Six). *Begin instead with the section you find most interesting* or at that point in your outline where you feel most confident about the validity or completeness of your material. In fact, begin any place where it seems easiest to begin and where you would like to write.

3. Choose a small block or section from your outline and simply *scratch down a few phrases to stand for sentences.* In minutes you may find yourself quite unintentionally writing consecutive prose, and soon you will have a whole paragraph done.

4. Think of someone you know well and *write that person a letter* in which you try to explain your subject. The stigma of perfectionism does not seem to extend to informal letters, for they are by nature casual and improvised. Many people have tried this successfully and found themselves inadvertently writing their papers.

5. *Try explaining your subject and what you particularly have to say about it to your roommate or to someone else.* This will not actually get sentences down but may generate argument. Once

you feel active and aggressive about your subject, you can crash through the first-sentence block. Surprisingly often a student comes in with his paper and says something like "I want to know what you think about this. I tried to explain it to my roommate, and he made me so mad that I just had to get my ideas written down." But be careful of trying this technique with a week-end date, or you may find that you have lost a date to gain a paper.

6. When in real despair, take a section from your outline and the cards that go with it, make sure it is all in order, think it over, and then begin to *dictate it slowly and evenly into a tape recorder*. Once you have dictated a section you can play it back and scribble it down. Now that you have something written, the first-sentence block is broken, and you can hopefully write the rest in a less electronic way. (This gimmick is especially useful for students who speak better than they write and so have more confidence in their voices than in their pencils. I have often asked a student what in the world he thought he was saying in some clumsy and ambiguous paragraph or even in a paper, and he has explained what he meant in clear and even graceful sentences that would have made an excellent first draft of written prose if he could have got them down.)

The outline as catalyst

Although efficient writing requires some degree of outlining, you must not let the outline stultify your imagination as you write. Its purpose is to keep the organization of your material in front of you so that you are freed to concentrate your attention on expression and style. But don't make your outline into an irreversible dogma. After all, it is your creature: you brought it into existence and can do with it as you choose. It is important to remember this obvious fact because as you probably know already from experience, the process of writing tends to be creative in itself. It very readily gives birth to bright new ideas superior to anything in your outline, to a more comprehensive view of the subject's unity, or to a sharper insight into its implications. There is an analogy with the phenomenon of catalysis in chemistry, when a chemical reaction speeds up or alters simply by the presence of another substance (the catalyst) that itself remains unchanged. In writing, the act of expression often behaves like a catalyst, calling into being material quite different from that on your outline. How this happens no one knows. But that it does happen is not to be ignored.

If you are alert to the attractive possibility of writer's catalysis you will know how to exploit it when it occurs. I have read too many undergraduate papers that introduced toward the end an idea far more profound and significant for the subject than any that were actually developed. Either the student didn't recognize what he had come up with, or there was no time left to reorganize so as to focus on this good new idea, or else he felt some timid and hide-bound allegiance to the sanctity of his outline. Once you recognize that you have hit upon something good during writing, stop, think it out, then reshuffle the basic blocks of your outline as necessary to give this idea a favorable position. Reshuffling is minimally tedious and bothersome if you already have a flexible outline of the kind I recommended earlier in this chapter. Sometimes, of course, a bright new idea will come along just where you want it and thus necessitate no reorganization. No matter when the idea arrives, you will, if you are alert to the phenomenon of catalysis, find a way to recognize and use it. When this happens, "How do I know what I think till I hear what I say?" begins to make sense.

Points to remember

1. Use a method of disposition that suits your writing temperament and the nature of your material.

2. Beware of the Tower-of-Babel outline: it is often more stultifying than helpful.

3. Use the scratch outline only for very short papers.

4. For most papers, use a flexible three-step technique of disposition: sort your cards into blocks of material, order the blocks, then do a scratch outline for each.

5. Let enough of your outline show in the finished paper to orient the reader.

6. Avoid, when your paper is a comparison, the do-it-yourself and seesaw organizations.

7. Organize papers explicating texts by concepts, not by paraphrase.

8. Keep the perfectionist's block from wasting your time by taking specific steps to help you get the first few sentences down.

9. Be prepared to find bright new ideas being generated by the act of writing and make your disposition accommodate them.

Expression: the paragraph is the basic unit

CHAPTER FIVE

"Life's not a paragraph," says the poet E. E. Cummings. But it almost is. If you can write a good paragraph, you can write a good paper. In fact, you can write. For the paragraph and not the sentence is the basic unit of all writing: when you are composing you necessarily think in terms of the paragraph and not the individual sentence. The reason for this is that each sentence's meaning and effect is contextual, the result of its impact on the surrounding sentences. A vague little sentence like "This is all to the good" is by itself innocuous and mousy. In fact, it has almost no effect at all. But wedged into a context of long, heavily developed sentences of the kind Basil Richards favors, it can have a striking effect of deliberate simplicity and alert concession. It invites you to anticipate the opening of the next sentence: "But. . . ." As the skillful writer writes each sentence, he keeps one ear cocked for the sentence to follow while his other ear rings with the sentence just written; that is, he is hearing the paragraph. Because we cannot think usefully of single sentences outside the context of surrounding sentences, then, the paragraph is the unit of composition. That is what *a paragraph is: a group of related sentences that together explain or expand a single idea.*

Before telling you how to write good paragraphs, however, I want to demolish two extremely common misconceptions of the paragraph that make effective papers impossible.

Two heresies about paragraphs

1. "Dividing Into Paragraphs." Sometimes we hear even instructors using a variation on this phrase: "Interesting ideas but faulty paragraph division"; or "When you divided this into paragraphs you. . . ." The significant word is "divide." It implies the existence of a whole that the writer "divides into" parts. Further, it implies that the whole (the paper) exists before its parts (the paragraphs). Otherwise it could not be "divided into" them. Someone in the eighteenth-century French romance *Paul et Virginie* explains that the twelve segments scored on the rind of a particular melon she is about to cut up are God's way of showing a mother how to serve a melon to a family of twelve. Whether this is true of melons or not, it is untrue of papers. A paper does not come into existence like a melon or a pie or a sheet of metal—as a whole that can be divided into parts. Instead, it *becomes* a whole by being built up cumulatively from those parts. As you write any paper you necessarily write paragraph unit by paragraph unit. You could not write it any other way.

This may sound like a quibble of terminology, but it isn't. For if you *think* in terms of dividing into paragraphs, then you will begin to lop off or prolong paragraphs arbitrarily. A writer who looks at the paragraph he is writing and says "This looks like enough" or "This is too short for a paragraph" or "I'd better start a new paragraph" or "I wonder if I could stop here" is, in fact, thinking in the unrealistic terms of dividing into paragraphs. His approach to writing is consequently impressionistic and even chaotic. If, instead, he thought of each paragraph as a group of related sentences organized around a key idea, then the question of division into paragraphs could not come up. He would have already defined and limited the scope and development of the paragraph before he began writing it. When he had achieved the purpose he had intended for that unit, he would know that his paragraph was complete.

2. *"Too Many Paragraphs": The Visual Heresy.* I once received from a freshman a two-page paper boasting no less than fourteen paragraphs. It did not read coherently, of course, because it contained no true paragraphs. Instead there were fourteen two- and three-sentence units. But held at arm's length, it looked all right. Each page, in fact, looked not unlike a page of book print that happened to contain seven short paragraphs. Of course, a page of print may contain more than twice as many words as a page of typing. This freshman, like many other un-

skilled writers before him, simply used the appearance of a printed page as a guideline to making paragraphs.

Here is the first page of a similar freshman theme:

"America the Beautiful! America is scored with highways, which are lined with hot-dog joints, flashing with neon lights, desecrated by car graveyards, and traveled only to reach the vast, tasteless, anonymous communities of ranch houses spreading like a great growing mold over our land."

Those are fighting words. The author implies that America, once beautiful, has been ruined by Americans. But he is judging only by what he sees: he is arguing against America from a visual standpoint only.

Car graveyards may not be everyone's cup of tea, but for those searching for spare parts, they are a great boon. Nevertheless, they are an enormous waste of materials. Why not crush them up and reuse the materials? This ought to be required by law.

If we are going to have a free enterprise system in America, we have to pay either the price of uglification, or the price of educating everyone to have good taste. This will mean a big program of art classes in the schools, because the consumer must be trained not only to insist on but to create an environment which is beautiful.

As for public health, aren't ranch houses healthier than many other forms of housing? Teepees may have been here today and gone tomorrow, and therefore preserved the landscape, but ranch houses are far more comfortable and healthful.

Also, hot-dog stands and hamburger drive-ins are a welcome sight when you are driving late at night and start to feel hungry. . . .

I used to write simply "too many paragraphs" at the end of such papers, but I don't any more. If a paragraph is really what I have said earlier that it is—a group of related sentences that expand or explain a single idea—then a writer can scarcely have "too many paragraphs." If he really did, I would logically have to write "Your paper is too long" or "You have too many ideas." Rather, the reason for a proliferation of short paragraphs is most often not that the writer has written too much or has too many ideas (such papers usually say very little) but that he doesn't know what a paragraph is.

When I receive such a paper I look for one of two explanations of its paragraphing. First, I suppose the writer does know what a paragraph is. Then the fragmented appearance of his page may conceal a structure of true paragraphs underneath. He may have presented three real paragraphs in such a format that they look like nine but in thought and development are actually still three. The solution, of course, is very easy: the three true paragraphs are there and need only to be presented as such by retyping.

Second, if no true paragraphs are visible under the surface of fragmentation, then I know that the writer is innocent of any viable conception of the paragraph and that we will have to work on it. Like the freshman theme above, the paper will present, in "paragraphs" of two or three sentences each, a series of tiny, underdeveloped ideas—many merely stranded details, others unsupported and crumbling generalizations. The effect is that of an anthology of miscellaneous notes, more or less related to the subject. If the goal of writing is communication, then such a paper is a disaster. Problems of disposition often lie behind this situation. But even a highly organized paper still fails miserably if its author has used his eye as a guide to paragraphing.

Problems of length

Three Guidelines.   What then is the right length for a paragraph? Of course there is no rule for this. In informal writing, paragraphs usually tend to be shorter than in formal writing. Three principles will give you some guidance:

1. You should ordinarily have *not more than two or three paragraphs to the typewritten page.* Look at your old papers. If you find yourself consistently having written more than two paragraphs to the page, then they can scarcely be properly developed. At times you will see reasons for ignoring this guideline, but it works well enough as a homely rule of thumb.

2. Never write a one-sentence paragraph merely because you have a point on your outline about which you have only one sentence's worth to say. Such a paragraph will only have a tongue-tied effect. Either abandon this lonely shred of information or find an appropriate home for it in some other accommodating paragraph where it will be a little less exposed. *The only valid reasons for writing a one-sentence paragraph are functional: as a transition indicating a major shift in the subject or a new division of a long paper, as a forceful summarizing gesture, or as a point of*

unusual emphasis. Actually, such one-sentence paragraphs are not properly paragraphs at all but single sentences set off by themselves so as to strike the eye and gain special attention. Obviously they achieve this best in a contrasting context of long, heavily developed paragraphs. Even then you had better not use them often, or familiarity will stale the effect.

3. *Don't think of paragraphs as bite-sized pieces of information* made that way for the convenience of the nibbling reader. After all, readers have been known to read paragraphs of ten or fifteen sentences or more without fatal mental injury as long as those paragraphs were written clearly. Moreover, the bite-sized-pieces approach will lead you into one of the two heresies I have just sought to suppress. Even long, solidly argued paragraphs are infinitely easier for a reader to digest than the miscellaneous collection of tiny fits and starts produced by the visual heresy. So think of each paragraph not as a convenient bite-sized piece of information but as a further stage of your paper's realization, one more essential point of its argument or explanation. The criterion for judging the validity of each paragraph is not its length but its usefulness in the total context of the paper.

The Transfer from Outline to Paragraph. When you look at your outline (or at a single block of it if the paper is large or you have a lot of material), you will see a number of basic points. Each point will control a certain amount of subsidiary material: illustrations, arguments, quotations, details, qualifications, etc. Should each of these points become a paragraph? The answer depends simply on the amount of material available per point or the degree to which you wish to expand the point. If a point takes the form of a single statement about which you have nothing more to say, it should not become a paragraph at all. Otherwise it would appear as one of those tongue-tied one-sentence paragraphs already recommended for oblivion. If you have enough material to make at least four or five substantiating sentences for a point, then it sounds as if that could make a good individual paragraph. If you find yourself with a great abundance of material under a single point, however, the paragraph might be very cumbersome. Obviously, paragraphs that run to more than a page are hard for the writer to control. In such cases the wise procedure is to subdivide or reclassify this material into several subpoints, each one of which can become a paragraph.

Four essentials for good paragraphs

The technique for composing good paragraphs can be reduced to four essentials. Any paragraph worth reading must

1. be founded on *a topic sentence;*
2. develop in *an evident progress of thought,* usually to or from the topic sentence;
3. keep the reader oriented to that progress of thought by the use of *connective and transitional signposts;* and
4. keep the reader aware of the place of the paragraph in the larger context of the paper by the use of some *indication of function.*

1. The Topic Sentence.   This sentence is the core of the paragraph: it tells in a single statement what the paragraph is about. Sometimes it may actually summarize its paragraph. Although it need not be the most forceful or colorful part of your paragraph, it is the most essential. Where do you find it? Unless something very queer is going on, it will be in your outline as the point you wanted to make at this stage of the paper. The position of the topic sentence varies. Most commonly it begins the paragraph or perhaps is the second sentence. This forthright no-nonsense position has the advantage of orienting the reader at once.

Archaeology is uniquely dependent upon catastrophe. The small vocational accidents it shares with every other field. Sir Arthur Evans found a bead which happened to be Cretan, Schliemann heard a drunk reciting from the *Iliad,* and thus they were each inspired to make a great archaeological discovery: Evans found the palace of Knossos, and thereby uncovered a forgotten Cretan civilization, while Schliemann discovered the site of Troy. But in archaeology it is the major calamities that are preservative. If an ancient civilization was rich, its material remains have likely been looted. If, however, there was a disaster—an earthquake, a volcanic eruption which covered everything with lava—the preservation of most of the artifacts is insured. This is what happened at Knossos and at Pompeii.

But often a forceful topic sentence, especially if it summarizes, will achieve even more force when it concludes the paragraph; that is, the paragraph builds up to it.

When as a small boy Schliemann heard a drunk reciting from the *Iliad*, he was convinced—as contemporary scholars were not—that the poem was true. Later, he discovered the site of Troy. Sir Arthur Evans found a bead in Greece, and went on to discover the Cretan palace of Knossos, thereby revealing a previously unknown civilization. These small vocational accidents happen in every field. But in archaeology it is the major calamities that provide the major breakthroughs. Earthquake, as at Knossos, and volcanic eruption, as at Pompeii, insure the preservation of most of the artifacts of a culture. *Thus archaeology is uniquely dependent upon catastrophe.*

Both these positions make it very clear what the topic sentence is. But it may also lie somewhere inside the paragraph, exerting an orienting influence but not necessarily drawing much attention to itself.

In many admirable paragraphs a topic sentence as such will not appear at all. For undergraduate writers, however, it is wisest to make such a sentence an evident part of each paragraph by placing it at the beginning or at the end. Such placement can create a bold, architectural beauty of structure. Above all, no matter how you use your topic sentence, be sure that you have one in your disposition for each paragraph. Otherwise you cannot know whether you should have a paragraph or not.

2. Progress of the Thought.   The paragraph must develop. It must have an organization almost as if it were a miniature paper. A lot has been written on the various abstract patterns an organized paragraph may embody, including movement from cause to effect or effect to cause; comparison or contrast; extended example; division of the topic into parts; chronology, or order of events in time; description, or order of objects in space; extended definition; and others, including combinations of any of these. In fact, most complex paragraphs are such combinations. But much of the ink spent in expounding these patterns has been wasted, for most of us don't think of the paragraph we are about to write in abstract terms at all. Once you have the essential topic sentence and the material that goes with it, you don't ask yourself "Will I organize this by chronology? or by example? or by comparison?" The relevant pattern or combination of patterns springs naturally from the material and is in fact dictated by it.

Read the following topic sentences, for instance. Each suggests at a glance what kind of paragraph might follow it.

Leptis Magna and other abandoned Roman cities in the Libyan desert show what permanent disasters result from bad land management.

This topic sentence indicates a following paragraph moving either *from cause to effect* or *from effect to cause*. If from cause to effect, the progress would be from "bad land management" (cause) to declining agriculture to "abandoned . . . cities" (effect). If from effect to cause, the progress would be from "abandoned . . . cities" (effect) back to declining agriculture and further back to "bad land management" (cause).

The Ibo and the Hausa are as different as two African peoples could be.

Obviously, the paragraph to follow will be organized by points of *contrast*. (In paragraphs based on comparison or contrast you may use the otherwise forbidden seesaw and do-it-yourself methods of disposition; their disadvantages do no harm in the small paragraph format.)

An especially renowned industrial building by Frank Lloyd Wright is the Johnson Wax complex in Racine.

Here we expect a description of this building as an *example* of Wright's industrial architecture, with emphasis on the factors that make the building typical of his work as well as "renowned."

The Chinese government, by failing to cope with three grave and traditional problems, ensured the ultimate success of Máo's drive from the north.

Here the paragraph will necessarily be organized by *division of the topic* into its parts, the "three grave and traditional problems."

The rapid events of the last week of October 1962 proved the effectiveness of President Kennedy's decision to blockade Cuba.

This paragraph will follow the *chronology* of these "rapid events," and we will expect organizing words like "first," "next," "then," and "finally."

As you cross the harbor on the turnpike bridge going west, the pattern of New Haven's redevelopment suddenly catches your eye.

We expect this paragraph to provide a *description*, moving with the eye from background to foreground, from left to right, or from skyline to special buildings.

In the short history of depth psychology, few ideas have given rise to so much difficulty and controversy as Jung's concept of the "collective unconscious."

Obviously, the rest of the paragraph will contain a *definition* of the collective unconscious.

The only really valuable principle of paragraph organization, however, is this homely one: *make the thought of the paragraph go somewhere*. It should progress firmly, clearly, decisively. If this principle is too vague, implement it by the following strategy. Ask yourself where the topic sentence is to come—at the beginning? Then what kind of development will progress away from the topic sentence to expound it and to provide an opening for the topic of the following paragraph? Or is the topic sentence to come at the end? Then what kind of progress of thought will effectively lead up to it? (These basic lines of development often take the forms respectively of progression from general to particular or from particular to general, as in the paragraphs above on archeological accidents.) Then scratch down a little rough draft of the paragraph to see if it will work, thus applying the old principle of disposition. As is always the case with disposition, this outline of material will free you to concentrate on style as you write.

3. Connective and Transitional Signposts. Another way of saying that each paragraph demands a progression of thought is that each sentence in it must follow from the one before it. One very common fault in student paragraphs is the single sentence out of order, the sentence that breaks the progress of thought. Usually it contains no connective verbally relating its content to that of the preceding sentence. Connective and transitional devices are invaluable for two reasons. First, if you use them continuously you cannot really write a sentence out of order without seeing at once a flaw in the progression of thought; they force you to express verbally how the sentence you are writing relates to the sentence before it. Second, your reader needs them; they make it possible for him to follow at every step the progress of your thought—indeed, force him to comprehend its development. Connectives and transitions are to the reader what his master's footprints where the snow lay dinted were to Good King Wenceslas' page. As with disposition of the paper, so with each paragraph: you have flunked if the reader asks "How did we get here?"

There are three basic kinds of connective devices:

A. The repeated word or restatement of idea:
There has yet been no adequate description of some psychoses. The *psychotic* phenomena observed here. . . .

B. The demonstrative reference—*this, that, such,* etc.:
. . . who feared a sudden onslaught from England and France combined. In actual fact *such* an event was quite unlikely.

C. Pronouns referring back to nouns:
These demands were far in excess of those Chamberlain was willing to grant. It appeared to *him* that. . . .

Essentially the connective says "I'm saying *more* about this." The transition says "Now I'm relating a *new* idea to the foregoing." Strictly transitional words and expressions are very numerous and will come to mind automatically if the nature of the transition itself is clear to you. A few examples will suggest some of the kinds of transitions commonly designated in words:

Time:	*then, before, soon,* etc.
Place:	*beyond, below, next to*
Result:	*thus, hence, therefore*
Contrast:	*however, yet, nevertheless, but*
Addition:	*moreover, again, in addition*
Emphasis:	*in fact, indeed, certainly*

This is only a token list. Once you recognize the need to make the reader see signposts orienting him to the turnings of the thought, you will hit upon the right devices automatically. In fact, you cannot get on without them if you mean to fulfill the expository writer's basic aim of controlling the reader's comprehension at every point.

Note how connective and transitional signposts mark out the progress of thought in the following paragraph (connectives are marked [1] and transitions [2]).

Early in this century Theodore Roosevelt wrote that "the destruction of the Wild Pigeon and the Carolina Paroquet has meant a loss as severe as if the Catskills or the Palisades were taken away." *His*[1] words have an ominous ring today as *loss*[1] of animal species accelerates. *They*[1] apply to earlier ages *too*,[2] of course, for from the beginning the inevitable clash between man and animal has meant that in some places whole species would be killed off. There were once lions in Homer's Mediterranean, *for instance*,[2] wolves in Anglo-Saxon England, and salmon in the St. Lawrence. *These*[1] species survive elsewhere. *But*[2] many *others*[1] have slipped into the endless night of extinction. Back in the sixteenth century *that*[1] *night*[1] fell on the aurochs, the great wild ox of northern Europe, because its enormous size and curving, trumpet-like horns had made it for too long an irresistible target. Only the *horns*,[1] once used for ceremonial drinking vessels, survive ironically in Scandinavian museums. *Now*,[2] *however*,[2] new species come under the threat of extinction almost daily. (A world wildlife conference has listed more than 300 of *them*![1]) Of North American birds alone I need mention only the whooping crane, the California condor, and the Eskimo curlew. It begins to appear as if *their*[1] aeons-slow biological evolution and man's sudden and brilliant technological evolution are ultimately incompatible. *But*[2] it is *also*[2] worth remembering that, when a species dies out, it takes with it a unique set of genes that the *technology*[1] of *man*[1] can never hope to reproduce.

As you can see from this paragraph, not every sentence has to have a connective or transition; on the other hand, some sentences have both. But one of them must occur wherever there is a chance that the reader may lose the thread of the thought by failing to see how any sentence relates to the sentence before it.

4. Indication of Function. You should make clear how each paragraph relates to its immediate context, especially to the paragraph preceding it but perhaps to the whole paper or to a large section in a long paper. The topic sentence tells the reader what the sentence is about. *The statement of function tells him why he is reading the paragraph now.* Thus the statement of function relates paragraph to paragraph in exactly the same way that connective and transitional devices relate sentence to sentence inside the paragraph. Often the topic sentence, especially when it comes

at the beginning of a paragraph, will also indicate that paragraph's function.

A further source of discontent among prairie farmers lay in the
system of price supports for wheat.

This topic sentence, placed at the beginning of its paragraph,
tells you not only the special topic of the paragraph ("system of
price supports for wheat") but also how the paragraph relates to
the previous paragraph ("A further source"). Even without knowing the context, you recognize at once that this is one of a series
of paragraphs devoted to sources of discontent among prairie
farmers.

But, in spite of the strenuously applied official programs limiting
planting, cotton production increased yearly.

The "But" in this first sentence of a paragraph shows immediately
that its relation to the preceding paragraph is contrast or maybe
even contradiction.

The indication of function is of course not necessarily or even
usually a sentence. Often (as above) it is just a phrase or a single
word. The important thing to remember is that you need it to
keep the reader oriented and the material controlled. To do so
you had better make it a practice to *indicate function at the very
beginning of each paragraph,* whether or not the topic sentence
is to be placed there. If it is placed there, indication of function
and topic sentence will likely merge into a single sentence.

Andy Adamson on the inner city

To see how these four essentials of good paragraphs work together, read the following excerpt from a sociology paper on
urban-renewal programs, written by Andy Adamson as a junior.
The five paragraphs here, taken from the first part of the paper,
explain as background the development of modern urban poverty and the Inner City. I have used footnote numbers to indicate where the four essentials occur:

1. topic sentence
2. progress of the thought
3. connective and transitional signposts
4. indication of function.

You will notice that (2) and (3) often coincide because connective and transitional devices usually mark out the paragraph's progress of thought and commonly provide our only way of seeing that progress. Notice also the position of the topic sentence in the first paragraph.

The hayseed, *then*,[4] used to be considered a poor country cousin of the city slicker whose affluence he was expected to admire. *Their*[2,3] story parallels the ancient tale of the town mouse and the country mouse: the country mouse visits the town mouse, envies the wealth of his larder, but finds it guarded by the dangerous town cat, and so returns to the country a poor but more contented mouse. *But*[2,3] the country mouse has *now*[2,3] come to the city and settled down in spite of the cat. The change has not made *him*[3] affluent, *however*.[2,3] *In fact*,[2,3] most downtown city dwellers today are minority-group, first- or second-generation *urban poor*.[1]

The phenomenon of *urban poverty*,[4] of course, is not new in America.[1] We have had *urban poverty*[2,3] of a sort from the foundation of our cities, and its early members gave us their share of great men—Benjamin Franklin, for example. *But*[2,3] the first slums (as we now know them) arose from the waves of nineteenth-century European immigration and the concurrent industrialization of the northern states. We read, *for example*,[2,3] of how jerry-built tenements, crammed with fugitives from the Irish famine, collapsed or burned in Boston and New York. *And*[2,3] the crusading photographs of Jacob Riis document appalling physical and social conditions which now hardly exist, due mainly to the development of labor unions and to enlightened legislation.

Nevertheless,[4] urban poverty in the nineteenth century, or even before the Second World War, differed from our urban poverty today, mainly because diverse people lived and interacted in the cities.[1] Even quite modestly endowed families employed several servants; the very poor shared schools with the better off; charity was largely personal; and many unskilled jobs brought very poor people into contact with those richer than themselves. *Most important of all*,[2,3] people known to the poor made the American Dream a reality by honest sweat and muscle-power, not by sweepstakes and the numbers game. *Admittedly*,[2,3] there were signs of the future; the race riots in east St. Louis in the first quarter of this century sound very familiar. *But*[2,3] the poverty of the Inner City as we now understand it did not then exist.

Three main factors produced *the typical Inner City*[4] as we know it today.[1] *First*,[2,3] there is middle-class migration by automobile to suburbs which the middle class developed by themselves and for themselves, one of their main concerns being the preservation of their real-estate investment. *Second,*[2,3] there is the migration of rural, largely minority-group poor to the cities. *Most of these migrants*[2,3] came from the grinding, share-cropper poverty of the South, hoping to find work in the big northern and western industrial cities. *But*[2,3] *their hopes*[3] were blasted by the simultaneous migration of northern industry to the South in search of lower taxes and cheaper labor, and by the *third*[2] main cause of the Inner City today, automation. *Its*[3] *effect*[2] on the almost totally non-union urban poor has been brutal, but less so materially than emotionally. The tab for their *material*[2,3] needs is now in the hands of the financially staggering city governments. *But*[2,3] the hope of the urban poor has withered, because the relief offered them generally aims at subsistence only, not at getting ahead.

This concentration and isolation of hopeless people[4] has produced an Inner-City milieu to which we grandly attach the ambiguous tag "cultural deprivation."[1] *If we mean*[2] by *it*[3] that the urban poor have no culture of their own—no customs, no established ways of life, no sense of solidarity, no feeling of loyalty to place, *then*[2] the *tag*[3] does not fit, because many of the urban poor in Harlem, South Chicago, and Watts have all of these things in some form and degree. *But*[2,3] *if by culturally deprived*[2,3] we mean deprived of traditional American assumptions about the dignity of work, the chance to improve one's lot in life, the need to be independent, *then*[2] the term fits the Inner City poor all too precisely. What *cultural deprivation*[2,3] means for *them*[3] is, simply, despair. The Inner City today is *in fact*[3] a whole section of society immobilized by *despair,*[2,3] relieved only by riots, violence, and, once in a while, someone's escape. The enormous effort required to swim out of *its*[2,3] stagnant backwaters into the mainstream of American life is the subject of Claud Brown's autobiography, *Manchild in the Promised Land.* A first-generation urban Negro, *Mr. Brown*[2,3] was raised partly in Harlem but mainly in reform schools. *These schools*[2,3] he credits with giving him his first hope and expectation of the traditional American kind. It was to restore just *this hope*[2,3] to the urban poor generally and to prevent an enormous waste of human ability that the programs of urban renewal were begun. *But*[2,3] it remains an open question whether even *these*[3] Herculean efforts have much chance of success.

Points to remember

1. A paragraph is a group of related sentences that together explain or expand a single idea.
2. To think in terms of "dividing into paragraphs" is fatal.

3. To use your eye as a guide to paragraphing is just as deadly.

4. Ordinarily two paragraphs are quite enough for a type-written page.

5. One-sentence paragraphs are valid only when functional.

6. The points on your outline offer a flexible guide to paragraphing.

7. Every paragraph must be founded on a topic sentence.

8. Every paragraph must develop in an evident progress of thought.

9. Every paragraph must orient the reader to that progress of thought by the use of connections and transitions.

10. Every paragraph must keep the reader aware of its larger role in the paper by an indication of function.

Expression: the beginning and the end

CHAPTER SIX

"A whole is that which has beginning, middle, and end." Aristotle made this statement about the abstract nature of things as they exist in time and space. You will notice that it says remarkably little about papers and does not mention paragraphs. Yet when I ask students why they write special paragraphs to begin and end their papers, over and over again they parrot some form of this quotation from Aristotle (which must be the only shred of that dryly precise philosopher's writing that still springs freely to everyone's lips). Or else they say that you have to have an introductory paragraph and a concluding paragraph because their high-school teachers so decreed. In both cases the appeal is to dogma: one must always write such paragraphs without any rational consideration of whether they may be useful or necessary.

The results of this uncritical subservience to the dogma of the introductory and concluding paragraphs strike home shockingly when you are asked to write a two-page paper and are told that three paragraphs are all you can properly develop in that space. If you really believe the dogma, you must confine everything that is not introduction or conclusion—that is, the body of your paper—to a single paragraph. This is silly, of course, but I have received many papers of just such proportions, each like a postage stamp in a great gilt frame. If it can produce such results, the dogma that introductory and concluding paragraphs are mandatory in every paper should be rescinded.

Introductory paragraphs

Introduction as Statement. Obviously some sort of introduction is necessary so that you can let the reader know at once what he is to read about. But this need not mean an introductory paragraph. In many papers all you need is *an initial sentence or two at the beginning of the first paragraph that states what the subject is.* Then proceed at once in the same paragraph to your first point: "This paper is about X. The first point. . . ." Not so baldly as that, of course, but it will serve as a model. A paper on Latin-American forms of government, for instance, begins like this:

In spite of its population mélange of indigenous Indians, mixed bloods, and colonial Spanish, the forms of government in South American countries tend to follow traditional European patterns of rule by juntas, dictatorships, or elected democratic assemblies. Government by military juntas, in Europe a pattern as old as the Roman triumvirates. . . .

Another paper, on the forces that make for good design in advertising, takes two sentences to state its subject, then begins with the first main point:

The primary function of all advertising is to sell, but one of its most important effects is that worked on our sense of design. Because good design does not necessarily sell the product, pressure for visually acceptable advertising usually comes not from the industries or the agencies but from such sometimes enlightened sources of power as city-planning commissions and turnpike authorities. For instance, the Boston Redevelopment Authority. . . .

This kind of introduction is clear, efficient, and honest. If firmly and attractively stated, it will please and interest the reader by its directness. It is certainly preferable to the introduction that says no more but nevertheless compulsively attempts to achieve paragraph form. Everybody knows from experience how agonizing and time-consuming it is to cough up a few sentences for an introduction when you really have only one sentence's worth to say. The labors of Hercules are nothing as compared to your efforts to avoid banalities and absurdities. And all the sweat and anguish shows. So ask yourself "Do I need an introductory paragraph at all?" If the answer is "No," then simply state your subject and begin to expound it.

Valid Introductory Paragraphs. There are occasions, of course, especially in the case of longer papers, when you need an introductory paragraph. If you have the material for it and if it will help entice and orient the reader, then write it. But the criterion is usefulness, not dogma. There are three main kinds of introductions that invite the paragraph format:

1. THE GENERALIZATION LEADING GRADUALLY INTO THE SUBJECT. Here the subject itself will often be stated as a topic sentence concluding the introduction. Unless you have real material or ideas on hand, don't attempt to concoct such an introduction out of thin air, for it is a mine field of potential absurdities. Among them is the extravagantly general claim; for example, "Tragedy has appealed to men in every age." (Has it? How do you know? Who cares?) Even worse is the vast generalization coyly qualified: "Tragedy has perhaps appealed to men in every age." (But then perhaps it hasn't; you can't have it both ways. The statement is self-neutralizing and means nothing.) Both generalizations give the impression that the writer is scared of his subject and is moving far away from it to get a long running start. Introduction from generalization works only when the specific subject of the paper benefits from being located in a larger context. In such a case your introductory paragraph orients the reader in the general category in which subject X finds a place. But don't invent such an introduction if your sense of the larger category is shaky. Nothing will damn your paper more quickly in a reader's eyes than a set of puffed-up generalizations that any child could explode and that you don't believe yourself.

For a crystal-clear example of an introduction proceeding from a generalization, read the paragraph below. It begins a junior's anthropology paper on the social and cultural insights implicit in three books by the contemporary Nigerian novelist, Chinua Achebe. (Another paragraph from this excellent paper appears at the beginning of Chapter One.)

Perhaps the best way to understand how a society hangs together is to watch it fall apart. Chinua Achebe's three novels—*Things Fall Apart*, 1959, *No Longer at Ease*, 1960, and *Arrow of God*, 1964—provide a poignant account of the destruction of traditional Ibo society under the impact of British colonialism. Supplemented by occasional anthropological observations, Achebe's work is useful for insight into both the nature of traditional Ibo life and the mechanism of culture contact.

The following introductory paragraph begins a sophomore paper in which Basil Richards argues that the idea of tragedy underlying three contemporary plays is entirely novel and a complete break with tradition. In his introduction he works to arrive at a generalization about that tradition by looking back to tragedies of Sophocles and Shakespeare (read earlier in the same course). This generalization, brought into the open in the second-last sentence, gives him a useful context within which to begin the main argument of his paper.

In spite of the great distance separating Greek and Elizabethan culture, the tragedies of Sophocles and Shakespeare have many features in common. For instance, both demand as hero a noble and powerful man on whose life many lives depend. Oedipus and Lear are kings; Hamlet is heir to Denmark's throne; and Othello is so indispensable that the Venetian state suspends its laws to make allowance for his private actions. Once the tragic action gets under way, the hero usually gives evidence of a divided mind, its rational part struggling to fend off the very catastrophe that its instinctive and irrational part longs to embrace. Rational warnings that they are pursuing self-destructive courses only make Oedipus and Lear more determined to pursue them. Finally, at the end of these old tragedies there is usually a moment of calm when the shattered and humiliated hero begins to learn the hard lessons that disaster teaches him. Oedipus learns that there is no greatness so great as humility, Lear that the kings and kingdoms of this world are dust and clay. Classical tragedy, then, commonly offers the spectacle of a great man half-choosing the disaster that both destroys and informs him. But, when we attempt to find an equivalent spectacle in such modern and apparently tragic plays as *Death of a Salesman*, *Waiting for Godot*, and *Who's Afraid of Virginia Woolf?* it seems to have undergone a profound metamorphosis.

2. THE PIECE OF SPECIFIC INFORMATION DRAWN FROM INSIDE THE PAPER. This kind of introduction often works beautifully, especially in subjects where some narrative, chronology, or description is involved. Take an especially interesting bit of information or an illustration you would ordinarily have included somewhere inside the paper and turn it into an introduction. If you do this artfully it will have an enticing, come-on effect. Essentially you are teasing the reader into seeing what the illustration could be part of. (Notice how many articles in such magazines as *Harper's*,

The Atlantic, and *The New Yorker* begin this way.) Such an introduction will normally end with a statement of the main subject. But handle this type with restraint; when flashy or cute it appears blatantly as a gimmick.

The following paragraph begins a student paper on the Bill of Rights.

Patrick Henry, a fearless nonconformist, called it "the most fatal plan that could possibly be conceived to enslave a free people." He was speaking before a full house of his fellow Virginians in convention and not on the subject of the Navigation Acts or the Stamp Act. Instead, he was describing the United States Constitution, a product of the best minds of his age: Franklin, Washington, Hamilton, Madison, Monroe, as well as some of the lesser lights, including Elbridge Gerry of Gerrymander fame. On the other hand, Henry may have been right, for the Constitution he spoke of had, as yet, no Bill of Rights.

The first appearance of the Bill of Rights in anything resembling its present form was in the English Bill of Rights presented to William III on his accession in 1688 after the Glorious Revolution. . . .

Note how the Patrick Henry anecdote, which might ordinarily have come at some point inside the paper, catches the reader's attention at once when made into an introduction and suggests that the Bill of Rights is an unsuspectedly interesting and even dramatic subject. Imagine how much less enticing the essay would be if it began with its present second paragraph.

3. FILLING IN THE BACKGROUND. This can be very helpful in certain papers, especially those with historical subjects or in which a controversy underlies the subject. It requires precise information, of course, but gathering it often assists the writer in seeing his main subject in perspective. Andy Adamson wrote an excellent term paper for his course in British history on the political philosophy of John Stuart Mill. As an introduction he wrote not about Mill but about the elements that contributed to political restiveness and made for social change in Britain after 1815. Only then did he announce his subject to be Mill, having first oriented us in what turns out to be the intellectual and political milieu from which Mill's thought springs. In this kind of introduction, however, avoid the attempt to trace every

idea back at least to Zoroaster. Background is not valuable for its own sake but only as it serves to illuminate the main subject.

In the following example, taken from a senior's history-of-music essay, introduction by background is not only appropriate but almost inevitable. The paper discusses some examples of contemporary organ-building as attempts to reconstruct the organs of the age of Bach. To show why such reconstructions are necessary, the writer uses his introduction to outline a pattern of rise and decline in the history of the pipe organ.

The danger of continued development for any invention after it has reached a state of perfection appears nowhere more clearly than in the history of the pipe organ. Although pious legend ascribes the building of the first organ to the early Christian martyr St. Cecilia, it certainly existed at a much earlier date in ancient Egypt and Greece as the *hydraulos*, a portable organ blown by water power. During the Christian centuries, however, the organ did become more and more the instrument of worship, with its development paced by the requirements of liturgy. By the end of the seventeenth century it reached its peak in Holland and North Germany as the baroque organ—capable of effects brilliant or subtle but always clear-toned and articulate. The early eighteenth century saw the baroque organ's golden age, epitomized by the coincidence of Arp Schnitger's glorious organ-building with the almost unbelievable composing genius of J. S. Bach. After this, the organ had nowhere to go but down. During the nineteenth century it underwent perversions to make it imitate the then developing symphony orchestra: its tone was muddied, its articulation romantically blurred, its subtlety surrendered to theatrical effects, its pipes boxed up in dusty chambers. In the first half of our century the organ's reputation, understandably, reached its nadir. But at the same time efforts began to be made to rediscover the principles and techniques underlying Schnitger's lost art. By now these efforts have enjoyed success to the extent that we appear to have passed the threshold of a great renaissance in organ building. In this paper I wish to show how the new classical organs of the Dutch builder Flentrop, the Dane Frobenius, and the American Walter Holtkamp represent a recovery of the instrument in a modern form of its golden-age baroque glory.

The Straw-man Introduction.   I mention this because so many desperate students attempt it. Here is what happens. To give a paper focus you assert forcibly a position contrary to the one you intend to take. "It is too often said that. . . ," "Scholars have long believed that. . . ," etc. Never attribute these assertions to any namable man, however, and by no means give any references. No details allowed, either; that is one of the rules. You have in fact set up an anthithesis that luckily just happens to be opposite your thesis. Now come on with your big guns—heavy documentation and out-flanking note-cards. You can easily blast this no-good, straw-man scarecrow right out of the cornfield. Total defeat for "they," "some," and "it is commonly thought." Heroic author rides in triumph under hurriedly completed arches. Greeted by Miss Nubile Universe, given freedom of the city, ticker-tape parade, jets to Rio, other rewards too pleasant to mention. . . .

You can fill in the rest to taste. It is an ordinary wish-fulfillment fantasy—fun but arbitrary and unreal. So is the straw-man introduction. It is too easy to do and very obviously fixed. It makes you appear someone you probably aren't: a mature scholar who knows the ins and outs of his whole discipline. If you aren't, then leave the manufactured straw men, clay pigeons, and sitting ducks alone. Otherwise you will make your reader suspicious of your genuine material. This is not to say that you cannot use your introduction to explain a contrary position that you are prepared to demolish. But it must be a real position, held by men with names and admitting of documentation.

Here is an example of such an introduction legitimately used. It begins a freshman paper attacking the idea of civil disobedience. Notice how the writer explains the idea sympathetically and then says firmly and honestly that he is going to attack it.

"If the injustice is part of the necessary friction of the machine of government, let it go, let it go: perchance it will wear smooth. . . . But if it is of such a nature that it requires you to be the agent of injustice to another, then, I say, break the law." This is the central concept of Thoreau's essay, "Civil Disobedience," written in 1848. Since then, many struggling social leaders have used this powerful political weapon, especially in the form of passive resistance. Most notable, of course, are Gandhi and Martin Luther King; their results —an independent India and long-awaited civil-rights legislation— have been spectacular. Despite its admittedly desirable attainments, however, I will attempt in this paper to show that Thoreau's doctrine is politically and socially dangerous. I will concede at once that a democracy may be sometimes no more than the tyranny of a deluded majority (as de Tocqueville said and Thoreau himself implies). But, if each man's conscience must always be for him an authority higher than any in the state, then the result for the state must be anarchy.

Final paragraphs

Concluding paragraphs are better termed final paragraphs, for they do not necessarily express conclusion in the logical sense. Of course, if the paper centers on an argument, then the final paragraph will normally clinch that argument. But too often an undergraduate paper declines into its terminal paragraph with "Therefore" or "Thus we see that" when not argument or proof but explanation, description, analysis, or commentary has been its nature. Such irrelevant and fatuously hopeful phrases suggest that the writer has not really understood the character of what he has written and, worse, that writing the paper has been for him one more meaningless exercise. Even if the reader has loyally hung on your every word, such a termination will lose him. So it is important to end your essay with an appropriate effect.

Do You Need a Special Final Paragraph? First, as with the introduction, ask yourself if it is actually necessary to end your paper with a special final paragraph. Have you anything special to end with? any reason for such a paragraph? If the answer is "No," then by no means feel obligated to attempt one. Stop when you have finished what you have to say. But don't disappear over a cliff, like some old manuscripts that break off with a scribbled *desunt nonnulla*—"a lot is missing." For there should be a sense of decisive completeness in the last sentences of your paper even though you have no special final paragraph and are simply mopping up the last major point. If you have *reserved some important segment of your material for the end*, you will have no trouble ending firmly and easily without the labor of writing a final paragraph. But make sure you end as if you intended to.

The Flashy Peroration. In the intricately structured oration taught in classical rhetoric, the final section, called peroration, delivered a ringing recapitulation of the essence of the speech, full of emotional appeal. We are still familiar with this kind of conclusion from sermons, dramatized courtroom defenses, and senatorial rhetoric. When it works it is splendid, but when it misses by a hair it is bathos. Few of the phenomena of communication are sadder (or funnier) than a flashy peroration, intended to resound and to compel belief and action by that very resonance but instead ringing hollow and betraying its brassiness. One special form of this is the irrelevant terminal quotation chosen solely for its power of utterance. As a freshman I ended an incompetent essay on Walt Whitman by quoting Hamlet's eulogy of his father:

> He was a man, take him for all in all,
> I shall not look upon his like again.

Of course, this was slightly misleading: I had never looked on Whitman even once (if I had I would have been the world's oldest freshman), and could hardly expect to see him again. Besides being desperately irrelevant, pretentious, and silly, the quotation when applied to Whitman was ironic, raising problems that my ignorance sheltered me from.

Don't try to crank yourself up to synthetically ringing prose at the end unless the emotional appeal grows naturally out of content and tone. And don't end an ordinary self-respecting essay of explanation with an appeal to the whole world to join the crusade and anticipate the Last Judgment. Instead, bring your last point to a firm and rounded close, perhaps with some slight reference to the beginning of your essay. In most papers this will be a satisfactory and honest form of termination.

Valid Final Paragraphs. In some cases (particularly in long papers) you may require a separate final paragraph. If you do, make sure the nature of the paragraph is consistent with the nature of the paper. Three kinds of special final paragraphs are commonly useful in undergraduate papers:

1. PROOF ESTABLISHED. This closes appropriately any paper that is argumentative in nature. If the subject demands that you "prove" or "show" something, then the last paragraph ordinarily

will reassert the position defended and thereby clinch the argument. Here, for example, is the final paragraph of a freshman paper arguing against the introduction of socialized medicine:

As we have seen, the main purpose of a socialized medical program is to spread the whole cost of medical care either uniformly over a society, or according to ability to pay. Of the many arguments cited against it, the most persuasive of all, one which transcends all political positions, is that government control would hamper medical research. A national gift, such as a scientific bent for medical discoveries which alleviate enormous suffering all over the world, is a delicate thing. Whether socialized medicine and original research make comfortable bedfellows seems to depend upon national character. Sweden has married the two with success, whereas English doctors feel embattled, and many leave to explore research opportunities abroad. Would a form of socialized medicine work here? Yes, probably, if the program were carefully tailored for us. Whether Congress could draft and pass such delicately formed legislation on such a hot issue is another question. Even if it could, it seems to me that any program posing a threat to the progress of medical research is too dangerous to risk.

2. SUMMARY. At the end of long papers or papers with complex material or with several sharply separated sections, a summary of the central ideas will help to fix the main drift of the essay in the reader's mind. If possible, introduce a new twist, rephrase ideas, or organize the summary so that the paragraph avoids sterile recapitulation done as if by rote. In the paragraph below notice how the writer keeps summary from seeming mechanical by going on to introduce a new idea. The paragraph closes an education major's paper on the teaching tools used by the great innovator in primary teaching method, Maria Montessori:

Each of the peculiar Montessori teaching tools I have discussed—sandpaper letters, bits of velvet and silk, spools of thread, button frames, pails of water, soap, sponges, vegetables, geometric shapes, weights, puzzle maps, graded sticks, beads, beans, disks, flags, and nursery games like "Who can hear the pin drop?"—is designed to provide an independent learning experience which uses as much of the body and mind as possible. As I have shown, schools for small children are now only beginning to pick up these materials. But it is worth going one step further to note how many of them have been long ago copied by commercial toy manufacturers, and are available in corrupted forms in any good toy store today. The shoe-lacing exercise is popped onto a wooden shoe obviously belonging to the little old woman of nursery-rhyme fame; every baby can own a plastic mailbox in which to mail geometric blocks; the abstract puzzle map has been corrupted with place names but is to be seen everywhere. Because imitation is the highest flattery, it is only encouraging to see generally available even in corrupted forms the tools by which Maria Montessori so successfully taught small children observation, self-control, a sense of sequence, and skills—all of them prerequisites to further learning.

Short papers seldom require summary paragraphs, however, for in four or five pages the reader has little opportunity to forget any major point if you put it well in the first place. In shorter papers, then, do not use summary endings unless some special difficulty of the material warrants it. (Some students use summary paragraphs to give an illusion of order to an otherwise chaotic paper written out of the head. This eleventh-hour attempt to convince the reader that he and not the writer has been confused all along smacks of arrogance as well as slovenliness.)

3. IMPLICATIONS. This ending works beautifully in some kinds of papers, particularly those in history, philosophy, political science, economics, and sociology. It may easily follow a concluding proof or summary. Both proof and summary stop dead: they give an impression that the paper is self-contained. Implications, however, give one the feeling that the paper is open-ended, that the writer could convincingly extend his study to other areas. Moreover, by giving the author a chance to prove himself broad in his sympathies, they correct the narrow approach imposed by many topics. The last paragraph of Andy Adamson's paper on Mill, given below, develops as a movement outward from Mill's limited and cautious concept of democracy (the burden of the paper) to a lively and accelerating peroration in which Adamson presents some implications of Mill's political philosophy for the contemporary scene.

Finally it is necessary to say something about the applicability of John Stuart Mill for today. The first disproof one might offer of his fears for democracy is that democracy is still intact as a system of government. Intact in western countries, that is, those with strong and talented middle classes. Democracy has not worked and is not working in poorly developed countries, those with no middle class: Ghana, Tanzania, Laos—the list is long. And more specifically in the United States, the land of TV dinners and *Time* magazine, the voice of Mill speaks with many accents: with a soft socialist tinge when condemning HUAC for curtailing freedom of expression; with an Arizona or Los Angeles twang when condemning government interference with private enterprise; and with the accent of every thinking man when protesting against mechanical conformity in thought, speech, and action. And our form of government? Mill said, "It is the fact that one person is *not* as good as another; and it is reversing all the rules of rational conduct to attempt to raise a political fabric on a supposition which is at variance with fact." Pure democracy, like pure communism, can never be realized until all people become perfect. Until that time there will be a need for Establishments, Dictatorships of the Proletariat, Brain Trusts, New Frontiersmen. Even then our best is little better than a dumb show.

Notice how appeal here, though not devoid of emotion, nevertheless restrains emotion by stressing the idea of political reality: the effect is more intellectual and reasoned than emotional. Adamson has resisted the temptation to call his readers to join a crusade; instead he lets the implications imply. Notice too how he uses a quotation near the end. It is not dragged in extraneously, however, but presents a crucial point from the author he has been writing about and quoting all along.

What the king said to the white rabbit

You must not take away the impression that one of the kinds of introductory paragraphs described above will always be just right for beginning your papers and one of the final paragraphs for ending them. Instead, *ask yourself in the case of each paper whether an introductory or final paragraph would be useful and appropriate.* Avoid them unless you can tell yourself why you need them. The best possible advice about beginning and ending papers comes from *Alice in Wonderland,* where the King helps the White Rabbit to make a speech.

The White Rabbit put on his spectacles. "Where shall I begin, please your Majesty?" he asked.
"Begin at the beginning," the King said very gravely, "and go on till you come to the end: then stop."

If more writers would apply this bit of common sense to beginning and ending their papers, they would save themselves and their readers thousands of hours.

Points to remember

1. Write introductory and specialized final paragraphs only when they are essential.
2. A single statement will often serve as an adequate introduction.
3. When you must write an introduction, base it on generalization, a specific example, or background.
4. Avoid the straw-man introduction. Attack only real, documented positions.
5. Avoid the flashy peroration.
6. When you must write a special final paragraph, base it on proof established, summary, or implication.
7. Remember what the King said to the White Rabbit.

Expression: style and sentences

CHAPTER SEVEN

Style is the total effect of writing. It is the effect achieved by the ideas, the order, the paragraphs, the sentences, and the words all working together harmoniously. We recognize this in a negative way when we say about a writer "I don't like his style" and assume that we have thus consigned him to whatever underworld awaits flunking writers. The dismissal inherent in "I don't like his style" implies that style is not simply the clothes worn by the ideas but is part of those ideas and even inseparable from them. So when we make unflattering judgments about someone else's style, we are implying that we also do not like his way of thinking and indeed prefer not to read him.

The discussions of invention, disposition, and paragraphs in the preceding chapters, then, have concerned certain aspects of style. In this chapter and the next I deal with the two remaining aspects—sentences and words. Unfortunately, there is an embarrassing scarcity of workable techniques to help you manage sentences and choose words so that they contribute to good style. The reason may be that when you try to express your ideas in the best words, sentences, and sequences of sentences, a whole army of subjective human variables comes into action: personal factors, individual gifts, range of experience, reading background, discretion, sense of decorum, feeling for rhythm, and plain taste. Without these we would hardly have any writing at all and certainly no eloquent style, for style springs from just such individual sources. But the ways in which these sources affect the words and sentences we write are so diverse that hard-and-fast rules for the choice of words and the writing of sentences are almost impossible. The techniques suggested in this and the next chapter are simply a set of common-sense guidelines, none infallible but all directed to areas where, in my experience, students have shown themselves able to improve their management of sentences and their choice of words.

The stylistic instinct

There are fortunate people who, as they write, are able quite naturally to hit on the right word for the right place, to express a sense of speech rhythm, and to vary their sentences to control emphasis and meaning as they desire. In other words, they have rhetorical gifts (which usually, not always, coincide with high verbal-aptitude scores). Basil Richards showed evidence of these abilities from the beginning of his freshman year, although it took some effort to persuade him to develop them seriously and not as a means of verbal showing off. Such verbal abilities as Richards', whether disciplined or not, so often go along with a history of independent reading in school that they appear to result at least partially from that reading experience. People who have read regularly are not afraid of written English. It sounds as natural to them as speech. When they sit down to write they are likely to feel at home. (This does not mean that they necessarily write well without more training: consider Basil Richards' case again.)

If you don't have Richards' reading background, your situation is not necessarily bleak. You can still go a long way toward developing stylistic instinct by a crash program. I don't mean reading three books a day but rather making up through intensity what you lack in long experience. Try the following scheme one hour a day for a week or two.

The Copying Technique or Instant Reading Experience. Choose an author with a notably good expository prose style (not fiction). He might be a writer from the field of your academic major, but he should be modern. If you have no ideas, ask the instructor of your favorite course to suggest a good writer in his own discipline. Or else choose one of the following books, all on subjects of general interest and written by contemporary authors whose styles are attractive.

D. W. Brogan, *The American Character* (an English expert's articulate perception of the United States).

Loren Eiseley, *The Immense Journey* (an anthropologist's account of man's evolution for the layman).

Robert L. Heilbroner, *The Worldly Philosophers* (a lively study of the great economists).

Dwight Macdonald, *Against the American Grain* (informal, forthright, witty essays on men and books, especially the important essay "Masscult & Midcult").

Garrett Mattingly, *The Armada* (historical writing at its best).

Samuel Eliot Morison, *Admiral of the Ocean Sea* (Columbus' voyages by a naval historian who sailed the same course).

Sir Charles Sherrington, *Man on His Nature* (a famous account of the development of scientific attitudes toward the origin of organisms—premedical undergraduates especially will like this).

Edmund Wilson, *Apologies to the Iroquois* (conflict between treaty rights and the building of a power dam).

Virginia Woolf, *The Common Reader* (essays on literary subjects by a famous novelist).

You can find these in every college library; nearly all of them are in paperback. Now follow these steps:

1. Take a passage of a paragraph or two (not more than twelve or fifteen sentences) and read it over silently.
2. Observe the structure of the paragraph (i.e., the four paragraph essentials described in Chapter Five).
3. Read it aloud, listening to the stages in the paragraph structure.
4. Now copy the passage slowly by hand (don't type), one sentence at a time, reading each sentence aloud first and noting its pattern of emphasis and rhythm.
5. Now copy once more, typing if you like, trying to hear the sentences together in groups of two or three.

Although on the surface it may appear simple-minded, this exercise has helped many people develop an educated instinct for prose style and consequently a greater confidence and naturalness in their own attempts to write. By the time you reach Step 5 you will find that you have almost memorized the rhythm and scheme of emphasis in some sentences, even though you can't quite repeat the words. This is enough. The whole point of the exercise lies in sensing when sentences sound right. It marks the awakening of the stylistic instinct that guides most professional writers as they write. It is not particularly important at this point for you to be able to identify constructions and to name effects. No writer I can imagine would ever say to himself as he wrote, "Let's try a parallel construction here" or "I'd better suspend the predicate in this sentence" or "A double anapaestic rhythm would end this clause nicely." He may in fact do these things and many more. But it is his educated feeling for flexible style combined with his driving interest in what he is trying to say that automatically suggests to him ways of winning clarity, force, and grace. By no means would he distract himself from the job of writing to thumb through a series of abstract patterns and devices stored long ago in some corner of his brain and perhaps by now beyond recall. It will be necessary later in this chapter to identify some patterns of style while we work out rules of thumb, simply because we can't talk about anything without using names. But then we will be talking about style and not actually writing. My point is that the even moderately skilled writer does not explain his style to himself as he writes but feels and hears it grow out of his sense of his material.

Try the copying technique during a vacation or at the beginning of a term when pressures are low and most papers still lie ahead. Andy Adamson, whose reading background was as meager as most freshmen's, was persuaded to try it at the very beginning of his second freshman term. Although he had always thought of himself as unliterary, after two weeks of this exercise Adamson was surprised to recognize in himself stylistic aptitudes he never imagined he had. With his ear attuned to other writing, his own writing began to sound less forced and more natural.

Two elementary causes of monotonous style

At the very beginning of Andy Adamson's freshman year he presented me with two problems of style that luckily are easy to correct. I have nicknamed them the sedative effect and the washboard effect. They occur so predictably in the writing of freshmen who have underdeveloped stylistic instincts (and this includes most freshmen) that I have simply learned to expect them.

But they also turn up frequently in the work of experienced writers who become sloppy or fatigued. If you look back to Chapter One you will find both of these problems duly memorialized in Adamson's Errors List.

1. The Sedative Effect: A Series of Sentences of the Same Length. When a reader reads two sentences of the same length and then another and another, his ear grows dulled by the regular metronomic sameness. Each sentence unit begins to sound like the other sentence units, just as when you count imaginary sheep to make you doze off, each sheep looks identical to all those that jumped the fence before it. Read the following paragraph out loud.

(1) The cactus family is full of species brilliantly adapted to desert conditions. (2) In most of these species each part is specially evolved to catch and keep water. (3) Underground, for instance, the roots fan out shallowly to take advantage of the least shower. (4) Above ground, fleshy swollen stems act as reservoirs to store this water for long periods. (5) On the stems' surface a layer of wax—the cuticle— seals the water in. (6) Protruding from it are spines formidable enough to keep thirsty animals away. (7) These spines supplant ordinary flat leaves, which would allow a fatal amount of evaporation. (8) Finally, the number of stomata or pores for transpiration is cut to the minimum. (9) Such special adaptations enable cacti to thrive where other plants would shrivel.

This is the sedative effect. The reader may not actually snore under the impact of sentences following each other in this regular metronomic rhythm, but he will certainly begin to understand less than he should. Worse, he will be bored.

Sentences producing the sedative effect are almost always more short than long. In long sentences, the sameness of the sentence units does not come across to the reader so forcefully, although if it is there, sedation will eventually result. Once your sedative powers have been pointed out to you, the remedy is obvious: vary the lengths of your sentences. For freshmen who are afraid of writing and have shown themselves virtuosos in the art of boring, I sometimes suggest the following homemade temporary rule: *if two consecutive sentences are of the same length, the third must not be.* To keep it from being too mechanical and mindless, apply the rule by reducing one or two less important sentences to the status of subordinate (dependent) clauses for which a more important sentence becomes the main clause. This larger unit will break the sedative rhythm. Read aloud the following version of the cactus paragraph.

(1,2) The cactus family is full of species brilliantly adapted to desert conditions, with each part specially evolved to catch and keep water. (3,4) Underground, for instance, the roots fan out shallowly to take advantage of the least shower, while above ground, fleshy swollen stems act as reservoirs to store this water for long periods. (5) On the stems' surface a layer of wax—the cuticle—seals the water in. (6,7) Protruding from it are spines, formidable enough to keep thirsty animals away, and supplanting ordinary flat leaves, which would allow a fatal amount of evaporation. (8) Finally, the number of stomata or pores for transpiration is cut to the minimum. (9) Such special adaptations enable cacti to thrive where other plants would shrivel.

2. The Washboard Effect: A Series of Sentences Beginning with their Subjects. Some rural gravel roads develop distressing formations called "washboards"—a sequence of little iron-hard ridges, crossing the road each about a foot apart and giving every car that passes such jolts that it seems about to fall apart. Inexperienced writers give their readers similar discomfort by beginning many consecutive sentences with their main subjects. Read the following paragraph out loud, noting how, by the time you reach the fourth sentence, the sentences begin to come unstuck and to pull away. As a result, the individual sentence and not the paragraph becomes the unit of thought.

(1) One of the technological steps required to begin the long descent to the Civil War was the invention of the cotton gin. (2) A chain of coincidences lay behind its invention, beginning in 1792 when Eli Whitney graduated from Yale and found himself jobless. (3) He stayed for a while during that summer as the guest of Mrs. Nathanael Greene, a wealthy widow and owner of a plantation near Savannah. (4) He filled in the time there by devising gadgets to make housework easier. (5) Mrs. Greene, much impressed, introduced him to a group of plantation owners who hoped to separate cotton seeds from the lint by machine. (6) Whitney, in a few weeks, proffered a model capable of cleaning fifty pounds of lint a day. (7) He patented the cotton gin two years later and struggled thereafter to meet the demand. (8) The cotton gin had suddenly made quick fortunes

possible in the South. (9) Planters could now grow vast acreages of cotton as a cash crop, provided, of course, that they had plenty of cheap slave labor to keep costs low. (10) The ancient institution of slavery all at once assumed a powerful new importance as a result, and the firing of the first guns on Fort Sumter became a possibility.

Each new sentence here opens with an iron uniformity of design, and the prose, like the road, jars. If the reader grows edgy, his reaction is understandable.

The cure for the washboard effect is the same as for the sedative. Make it a rule *never to write more than two consecutive sentences beginning with their subjects,* unless you can see a good reason for doing so (such as deliberate parallelism or staccato-like emphasis). When you find yourself afflicted with the disease, treat it by finding inside some of the relevant sentences elements that are mobile in position (such as adverbs, phrases, and subordinate clauses). Move them to the beginning of the sentence to vary the effect and break the washboard rhythm. Read aloud the corrected paragraph below, noting how the sentences dovetail to make the whole paragraph the unit of thought.

(1) One of the technological steps required to begin the long descent to the Civil War was the invention of the cotton gin. (2) Behind its invention lay a chain of coincidences, beginning in 1792 when Eli Whitney graduated from Yale and found himself jobless. (3) During that summer he stayed for a while as the guest of Mrs. Nathanael Greene, a wealthy widow and owner of a plantation near Savannah. (4) There he filled in the time by devising gadgets to make housework easier. (5) Mrs. Greene, much impressed, introduced him to a group of plantation owners who hoped to separate cotton seeds from the lint by machine. (6) In a few weeks Whitney proffered a model capable of cleaning fifty pounds of lint a day. (7) Two years later he patented the cotton gin and struggled thereafter to meet the demand. (8) Suddenly the cotton gin had made quick fortunes possible in the South. (9) Planters could now grow vast acreages of cotton as a cash crop, provided, of course, that they had plenty of cheap slave labor to keep costs low. (10) As a result, the ancient institution of slavery all at once assumed a powerful new economic importance, and the firing of the first guns on Fort Sumter became a possibility.

The sedative and washboard effects often occur together in the work of inexperienced writers, resulting in a kind of grown-up babytalk or primer style. Even Basil Richards, with his instinctive feeling for stylistic variety, was capable of lapsing for a paragraph or so into a succession of ten-word sentences, each beginning with its subject. (But Homer is also said to have nodded.) The main thing to know about these two problems is that they exist. Once alerted, you can easily avoid or remedy them.

The strategy of sentence variety

There is a classic dialogue between student and instructor that recurs in office after office, year after year, just about the time the leaves are falling. The student, squirming in his chair after an analysis of his style, is dying to change the subject. About this point in the afternoon he usually feels the need for a little praise. Even a couple of kind words would do. Actually, he had, in all due charity to himself, rather approved of that paper when he pulled it out of the typewriter last week. Anyway, he knows, as he has always known, that it isn't how you write that counts but what you say: that is the meaning of democracy. Getting upset about style is, he figures, mostly a hangover from an aristocratic age when people had time to bother about such things. So he says, as other students sitting in the same chair have said before him, "Look, I *know* I don't write too well. But, *apart from all that,* what do you think of my ideas?" To which the instructor replies, and *should* reply, "I can't understand your ideas apart from the way you write."

The instructor is saying that style is not ornament—nice if you have it but optional. He is saying that style is essential to writing anything. As we have seen, the blanket condemnation of a writer's ideas that is implicit in "I don't like his style" rests on just this assumption. But how are you to make this abstract principle work for your own prose?

Remember the well-loved sedative and washboard effects. Both are forms of rhythmic monotony in the handling of sentences. The result is monotonous style. To cure them you must transform that monotony into variety. But such variety by itself is elementary—a desperate cure for a desperately elementary problem. The next step is to make rhythmic variety also intelligent variety; that is, the rhythmic variety must express the variety of meaning and emphasis that a mind—your mind—has given to the material. To bring this down to the level of the sentence, *what you want a sentence to say and the importance you want it to have in relation to the sentences around it—these will determine the kind of sentence to use and its particular rhythm.*

But what are the choices?

The Varieties of Sentences. Here for a moment I must use some technical terms of grammar probably already familiar to you. Grammatically, the three basic kinds of sentences are distinguished by their clause structure as simple, complex, and compound. To illustrate these I will use sentences from a paper Basil Richards wrote in his junior year for a history-of-art course. Later, to show how these same sentences function together in context, I will quote the two paragraphs they come from.

The *simple sentence* has one independent clause:

In fact, the architect Longhena seems to have spent most of his energy devising the façade.

The façade of the Salute is a Renaissance restatement of the same theme.

The *complex sentence* has one independent clause and one or more subordinate (dependent) clauses:

While the inside of Santa Maria della Salute appears to languish in its static concord, the outside is in constant motion.

The *compound sentence* is two simple or complex sentences joined by "and," "but," "or," "nor," or "for."

To us it is the symbol of the perfect heavens untouched by the turmoil below, but to Longhena it was the crown of stars that, in the Book of Revelation, graces the head of the woman "clothed with the sun and with the moon under her feet."

Each of these types has its own special use.

The Normal Sentence. "What's the matter with those guys?" my graduate assistant complained after his first few weeks of teaching freshmen and reading their papers. "They seem to think every sentence has to be simple." He had run up against a wrong-headed notion that bedevils the writing not only of freshmen but of many people experienced enough to know better. Unlikely as it may sound at first, the normal sentence in good writing is not the simple sentence. If it were, it would hardly be possible to avoid for long the sedative and washboard effects, because the simple sentence, used generously, leads right to them. The only prose ordinarily based on simple or compound sentences, in fact, is the speech of children, Dick-and-Jane readers, and folk literature. In most prose, as you may have guessed by now, *the normal sentence is the complex*. Because the position of its subordinate clause is flexible, the complex sentence allows for more variety of rhythm and emphasis than the other two kinds can ever approach. This variability allows a reader to progress through a whole series of complex sentences (assuming that they avoid the sedative and washboard effects) without ever sensing monotony or sameness. Furthermore, the maneuverability of the subordinate clauses, which ordinarily contain the less important material, permits immediate control of emphasis, because the main or independent clause can have almost any place in the sun that you want to give it.

Sometimes a grammatically simple sentence has the effect of a complex sentence:

While the inside of Santa Maria della Salute appears to languish in its static concord, the outside is in constant motion.

This sentence is complex, with one clause subordinated to the other. The following version of the same sentence is grammatically simple:

While appearing inside to languish in its static concord, the outside of Santa Maria della Salute is in constant motion.

You can see, however, that it contains the same material as the complex version, that "inside" is still subordinated to "outside," and that most of the words are the same. The only substantial difference is that an elaborate prepositional phrase ("While appearing . . .") has replaced the subordinate clause. Lacking a subordinate clause, the sentence, in the strict grammatical sense, is simple. Because it has virtually the same effect as the complex version, however, you should for all practical purposes consider it a complex sentence.

The Specialized Sentences. These, of course, are the simple and the compound. Here I must reassert a principle touched on earlier: *the effect of a sentence depends on the context created by the preceding sentences.* Ordinarily, that context will be made up of complex sentences. Following them, a short simple sentence will be arresting and forceful and just right for drawing attention to important material. In three situations the emphatic simple sentence is invaluable: (1) to give a forceful summary statement to a point just made by preceding sentences; (2) to introduce a new point in its clearest, simplest form before you qualify and elaborate it; and (3) to indicate a new direction of argument or a paragraph subdivision. *Complex sentences for normal prose, simple sentences for emphasis*: that is the basic rule.

The *compound sentence* should occur least frequently. It is a highly specialized form, effective only when you have something naturally compound or coordinate to say. Properly used (as in the example from Basil Richards just given), it is almost like an equation, holding together in balance two clauses you want to give equal weight to. Their interrelation may be collective (so joined by "and"), alternative ("or"), or contradictory ("but"). The great value of the compound sentence, when you can justify its use, is its fine, formal, authoritarian ring. This is just right at certain moments. But many careless (and not unpublished) writers use it incessantly, even when their material cries out for complex sentences. It is much too easy, as well as childishly regressive, to fall into the sloppy, conversational habit of connecting clause after clause with "and."

Loose and Suspended Sentences. To increase the sources of useful variety, two other sentence patterns can be superimposed on the simple, complex, and compound grammatical patterns. Called loose and suspended patterns, they designate rhythm according to the order of word groups inside some sentences. In the *loose sentence* the author completes the basic subject-verb-object of the main clause and then, apparently casually, adds a string of modifiers.

From this vantage point we can appreciate the wise decision to keep the body of the church as low as possible, which permits an all-inclusive view while avoiding the discomfort of a dip in the Grand Canal.

With "possible," the basis of this sentence is complete; the other elements (beginning "which" and "while") are added almost as afterthoughts. And this is the special value of the loose pattern: it suggests informality, conversation, an author who is speaking easily and almost extemporaneously, feeling out his meaning in the presence of the reader. Notice how effective such informality is in the sentence above, which, with its "we" and its touch of humor at the end, attempts to make the reader feel as if he were in the author's company and looking from the "vantage point."

The *suspended sentence* (often but less descriptively called *periodic*) operates on a much more formal principle, by deliberately interrupting the main subject-verb-object structure. The interruption compels the reader to keep the earlier part of the sentence in his mind until the end of the interruption, otherwise the sentence will not make sense.

This collection of geometric solids, which Longhena crocheted together with a string of cornices, balustrades, and brackets, produces from the distance an extremely varied and interesting silhouette.

Because we wait until the very last word for the completion of the basic subject-verb-object unit, a great deal of emphasis develops at the end of the sentence; this is proper because "extremely varied and interesting silhouette" sums up (as you will see) the development of the paragraph to this point. In this sentence the writer stands apart from the reader; there is no illusion of chummy joint investigation. Instead, the writer appears to know dogmatically what there is to say and by presenting the whole suspended sentence as a single unit, seems to demand that the reader accept the whole idea it contains. You will notice too that the suspended sentence structure lends itself beautifully to the idea of "crocheting together," as in a web.

The effect of the suspended sentence is to say "Now hear this," while the loose sentence says something like "Let's figure this out." It is the difference between the grandeur of authority and thoughtful persuasion. Not every sentence is either loose or suspended, however. Both are special rhythms, useful for embodying particular kinds of information. Ordinarily, of course, the suspended pattern is more emphatic and declarative. Loose and suspended sentences coexist with the three grammatical patterns: a complex sentence, for example, can also be loose or suspended or neither. The range of combinations offers an extremely flexible means of variation.

Basil Richards on the churches of Italy

To see the various rhythmic possibilities at work together in continuous prose, read the following two paragraphs (from which I draw the examples given above). They come just before the final paragraph of the paper mentioned earlier, which Basil Richards wrote for a course in the history of art. In it Richards compared two famous old Italian churches one thousand years apart in construction, San Vitale in Ravenna and Santa Maria della Salute in Venice. In these paragraphs Richards, who has just analyzed San Vitale and the interior of the Salute, now turns to the latter's exterior. As you read, note the shifting of sentence rhythms to reflect the particular meaning and relative importance of each idea.

(1) While the inside of Santa Maria della Salute appears to languish in its static concord, the outside is in constant motion.   (2) In fact, the architect Longhena seems to have spent most of his energy devising the façade. (3) Even from some distance away we can see that the basic units of the exterior are the six aediculae, the triumphal arch, the bema dome flanked by two slender campanili, and the magnificent crown surmounted by an airy sculptured lantern.   (4) This collection of geometric solids, which Longhena crocheted together with a string of cornices, balustrades, and brackets, produces from the distance an extremely varied and interesting silhouette.   (5) But the near view offers a very different visual experience.   (6) For, when we gaze at the Salute from its bank of stairs near the shallow square that ex-

Sentence 1. Complex. Topic sentence introducing new subject for next two paragraphs ("outside"). Reference to "inside" orients reader to what has gone before (indicative of paragraph's function).

2. Simple. Emphatic after complex. Introduces subject of present paragraph, "façade."

3. Complex. Loose. Information about façade.

4. Complex. Suspended. First half of paragraph, on façade as seen from a distance, ends here. Emphasis on "silhouette."

5. Simple. Draws attention to new division of paragraph subject: "the near view."

tends to the water, all that is visible is the ornate entrance connected to the drum by roller-coaster buttresses and the glistening dome. (7) From this vantage point we can appreciate the wise decision to keep the body of the church as low as possible, which permits an all-inclusive view while avoiding the discomfort of a dip in the Grand Canal.

(8) More significantly, the exterior offers documented proof of the architect's sensitivity. (9) When, earlier, I discussed the Byzantine church of San Vitale, I emphasized the kinesthetic effects achieved by surrounding the tranquil nave with an oscillating ambulatory. (10) The façade of the Salute is a Renaissance restatement of the same theme. (11) In this case, however, the architect, using a highly original vocabulary in a unique context, has cleverly concealed the octagon and drum of the church behind a forest of sculpture and peculiarly Baroque forms which emphasize the relation to the human figure. (12) The convoluted surface, sheathed in bands of light and dark, contributes further to this metaphor of man's mortal existence; and above it all, sitting masterfully astride the confusion, is the simple ogival dome. (13) To us it is the symbol of the perfect heavens untouched by the turmoil below, but to Longhena it was the crown of stars that, in the Book of Revelation, graces the head of the woman "clothed with the sun and with the moon under her feet." (14) Because this contrast is expressed without rather than within the building, the staging may reflect the change in religion from an inward-looking private affair to an outgoing public concern.

6. Complex. Rather loose. Conversational informal "we."

7. Complex. Loose. Very informal sense, as in (6), of author's presence as companion. (6) and (7) are both investigations.

8. Simple. Announces new aspect ("sensitivity") within larger subject of exterior.

9. Complex. Earlier information recalled.

10. Simple. More precise statement of paragraph's subject, as made possible by (9).

11. Complex. Suspended at beginning, loose at end. Suspension hints at developing formal manner.

12. Compound. Double suspensions. Good situation for compound because of parallelism in idea ("surface"/ "dome"). Note formal and symmetrical hour-glass shape of this sentence with a subject at either end. Also, a great deal of weight thrown on "dome," subject of the next sentence.

13. Compound. "To us"/"to Longhena": another ideal situation for a compound sentence.

14. Complex. Speculation. Reduced excitement. A return to normal.

In these two paragraphs the sentence rhythm expresses the character of the material. The first paragraph is largely information gathered, as it were, on the spot but set forth in an orderly series of steps as we draw closer and closer to the façade. Here the sentences are dominantly complex (five complex and two simple), reflecting the investigative and informational quality of the material, while the simple sentences, contrasting with the complex, mark out unmistakably the order of the paragraph.

The second paragraph, however, is not fact-finding but interpretative. As it reaches its climax, we feel imagination and even emotion at work. Here the sentence patterns are mixed (three complex, two simple, and two compound). While simple sentences once more serve to orient, the complex sentences do not make up a majority; there are just enough of them to remind us of the normal pattern. Against this, attention shifts to the unusual and contrasting compound sentences with their climactic, emotional perceptions. Then everything falls back to normal as the final ordinary complex sentence re-establishes in the ear its familiar dominant rhythm.

Together these two paragraphs contain fourteen sentences—eight complex, four simple, and two compound. The normal complex pattern yields only briefly in the second paragraph to permit a special effect. Everywhere the simple pattern draws attention to the order of the material and asserts basic subjects. If in your own writing you can *make sentence pattern reflect material by contrasting simple and compound sentences against a basis of the normal complex,* as Basil Richards has done here, you will have brought a key area of style under your control.

Common sense about emphasis

Take with a grain of salt the idea that emphasis is always a good thing. As we know, a carefully placed simple sentence is emphatic within a context of complex sentences only when it occurs infrequently. A whole passage of simple sentences could not possibly be emphatic, for the attempt to make everything emphatic is illogical. *All emphasis means no emphasis.* To be useful as a means of controlling the reader's understanding, then, emphasis, whether of a word in a sentence or of a sentence in a paragraph, must be scarce. Before you write a sentence or a paragraph, ask yourself exactly what it is you want to hit the reader with hardest and then make that, and that alone, emphatic.

Emphasis Inside the Sentence.   Some annoying people struggle to make every word emphatic:

And there it was! Right in the very densest part of that absolutely impenetrable spruce swamp I had practically stumbled on a really more than perfect specimen of the extremely rare *Orchis rotundifolia,* incredibly unusual so early in the summer.

We all know people who talk like this. It is hard for them to be emphatic when they really want to be, for they have already squandered their intensive golden words. Moreover, hysterical anxiety to convince tends to create scepticism instead. "The lady doth protest too much, methinks," says Hamlet's mother, as her counterpart in the play-within-the-play repeats and amplifies promises of undying love; and the proverbial gentleman from Missouri would sympathize with her ("I'm from Missouri: you will have to show me"). In the preceding extract, the author has insisted so much that as a result we automatically discount his statements; for example, how did he manage to penetrate "the very densest part of that absolutely impenetrable spruce swamp"? He means that the swamp is dense. But in view of the noise he makes throughout the sentence, it is impossible to tell what part of it he wishes to make important. By emphasizing everything, he cannot call attention to anything. Suppose he means to stress the earliness of the plant. Then he might bring that fact to the fore very simply by *putting the element to be stressed in the naturally most emphatic position—the end of the sentence.*

In the dense spruce swamp I had stumbled on a perfect specimen of the rare *Orchis rotundifolia,* particularly unusual so early in the summer.

Surely this will do better, with true emphasis where the author (we hope) wants it. The revision suggests that an effective, sane sentence can achieve emphasis where you want it without the promiscuous use of such intensifiers as "very," "most," "extremely," and their like. These are good English words, but they lose their virtue the moment they become common on the page. As with garlic, a little goes a long way. *Use intensifiers with restraint;* then they will be powerfully emphatic.

Although the end and to some extent the beginning of a sentence are the naturally most emphatic positions, changing a word from its normal position often serves well enough to make it emphatic. This is especially true of modifiers. If you wish to emphasize them, put modifiers in something other than their normal position. In the following sentence, for instance, the adjectives "small and weak" are in the normal position in front of the noun they modify:

This hawk's small and weak talons confine its attention to little animals.

But when we write

This hawk's talons, small and weak, confine its attention to little animals.

the two adjectives, which are essential here to the reasoning of the sentence, receive from the change of position a stress they did not have before. Such emphasis is subtler, more natural, and more convincing than pure verbal pounding, as in "This hawk's extremely small and very weak talons . . . ," which tends to make the reader suspect the soundness of the writer's knowledge: why does he protest so much? Make this a rule: *within the sentence, draw attention to the most important word by choosing its position carefully.*

Points to remember

1. Try the copying technique to give you some feeling for style.
2. Avoid the sedative effect by varying sentence length.
3. Avoid the washboard effect by varying the beginnings of sentences.
4. The effect of a sentence depends on the context created by the preceding sentences.

5. Use complex sentences for normal prose but simple for emphasis and compound for equations.

6. The loose sentence pattern is casual and familiar, the suspended is more formal and dogmatic.

7. All emphasis means no emphasis.

8. Use intensifiers with restraint.

9. Draw attention to the most important word in the sentence by choosing its position carefully.

Expression: *words, words, words*

CHAPTER EIGHT

"What do you read, my lord?"

"Words, words, words," replies Hamlet, closing the book in disgust.

The writer often feels the same way when he comes to the hardest and most crucial problems of style: finding the right word for the right place. He will hardly be comforted to hear Jonathan Swift saying, "Proper words in proper places make the true definition of style." A few common-sense principles will minimize the chaos of choosing and managing words and will put you as much as possible in control.

Right words and wrong words

Vocabulary. Because English has a teemingly rich vocabulary, it is only natural that teachers should expect students to acquire as much of it as possible. But a great deal of recent "vocabulary building" is rather shaky in conception. Knowing the meaning of a word will help when you happen on it in reading or speech, but meaning alone will not enable you to write the word correctly. One of the silliest things you can do is to flip through your dictionary looking for unheard-of words, which you then try to work into your paper so as to impress an instructor with your precocious literacy. Students who attempt this (Basil Richards tried it a few times) are asking for trouble. This is the rule: *use a word new to your vocabulary only when you have learned it in context, then checked its meaning in a good up-to-date dictionary*. When you come upon a strange word in reading, reread the sentence in which you found it to get a feeling for the word's special flavor and quality (its "connotation"). But because context can be ambiguous or misleading, don't rely on it for meaning. It is all to easy to guess at a new word's possible meaning and then assume you are right. Some people use a word wrongly, or comically, all their lives because even their best friends won't undeceive them. Toward the end of one of his more forceful sermons, a local college chaplain said: "We must, like Saint Paul, take up this challenge with enervated spirits." He had unfortunately assumed that "enervated" meant "strengthend" or "energized," whereas its real meaning is "weakened." No doubt he had learned the word in a context where "energized" would make plausible sense and had never thought to check it in a dictionary. If he had, he could have avoided saying the opposite of what he meant and being puzzled by suppressed titters from the pews.

Every student must have at hand an adequately inclusive dictionary. At the moment, the *American College Dictionary* (Random House), *Webster's New World Dictionary of the American Language* (World), and *Webster's New Collegiate Dictionary* (Merriam-Webster) are the best. Be sure to get the most recent editions.

Besides a good dictionary, there are two other invaluable books that every student should own. The first is H. W. Fowler's *Dictionary of Modern English Usage*, second edition, revised by Sir Ernest Gowers (Oxford: Clarendon Press, 1965). This edition of a famous British reference book, classic since 1926, now takes account of American usage as well. If you are in doubt about the usage of any word or phrase, check with Fowler. He will have anticipated your problem and solved it in the most concise possible way. For instance, you know the word "affinity" but can't remember whether it is followed by "with," "for," "to," or "between": all sound plausible to you. But not to Fowler. In a second he will tell you that it is properly only followed by "with" and "between" and why. The proper use of some words is a matter of opinion, even among experts. In such cases Fowler's opinion is always clearly argued, but you should be aware that he will favor conservative usage. Use *Modern English Usage,* then, as a criterion of the usage expected by a serious, conservative, tradition-minded reader.*

You must also have at elbow one of the many versions of Roget's famous *Thesaurus of English Words and Phrases,* indispensable since 1852. The *Thesaurus* (Latin for "treasury") groups synonyms and other words and phrases characterized by similar meaning. As with an ordinary dictionary, you should not ransack Roget searching out an outlandish word to supplant a familiar one. The proper use of the *Thesaurus* is to rescue you when the precise word you want won't come to mind: "It was on the tip of my tongue." In that familiar situation look up in Roget a word close in meaning to the one you want, and you will find listed along with it the word that has been eluding you. Even Basil Richards, with his verbal flair, could never get out a paper without Roget in the wings.

Verbs and Impotency. The English vocabulary is rich, and its richest part is its verbs. Julius Caesar could only say, when he invaded Britain, *"Veni, vidi, vici,"* but if he had stayed for a while he could have said "I came, I saw, I overcame" or "I arrived, I perceived, I conquered" or variations of those verbs. Not only does modern English have both an Anglo-Saxon ("come") and a Latin or Latin-French ("arrive") verb for almost every action, but it also has three different ways of putting the verb: "I come," "I am coming," "I do come." No other Western language has such facility with verbs.

Given this power of nuance in English verbs, it is astonishing how few writers use them well. One of the greatest curses of run-of-the-mill American writing, for instance, is its crippling dependence on the passive voice. (In the active voice the subject acts: "I struck." In the passive voice the subject is acted upon: "I was struck.") If you examine these two sentences, you will see what is wrong with the passive voice:

*See also *Modern American Usage: A Guide* by Wilson Follett, edited and completed by Jacques Barzun (New York: Hill and Wang, 1966). Because Follett covers Fowler's ground from a purely American point of view, you may find him a more accessible (and no less meticulous) guide to the usage of words.

An eagle dropped a turtle on Aeschylus' bald head.
A turtle was dropped by an eagle on Aeschylus' bald head.

The passive version is inferior to the active because (1) the natural energy of "dropped," suggesting action and surprise, diminishes in the slower and less direct "was dropped"; and (2) the passive verb necessitates a wordier, clumsier sentence that lacks tension. The passive version of the following sentence produces an even clumsier construction, like a nail hit obliquely by the hammer and bent, not driven in by a dead-on blow:

Controlled research does not verify the Oedipus complex.
The Oedipus complex is not found to be verified by controlled research.

And the clumsiness of the following construction is intolerable to any ear:

A dog ran across the street.
The street was run across by a dog.

It is precisely this passive construction that blights millions of pages of modern writing.

A typical example of a physical symptom produced by an inner tension may be found in six-year-old Kenneth. It could be easily seen that Kenneth's trouble had been centered in asthma. He was discovered to have an excessive fear of dirtying, and to be excessively neat. His mother could be considered to be over-affectionate, and to be possessed of a strong wish that Kenneth be kept dependent, while his father could be termed unreasonably strict. It is interesting to note that a great many of Kenneth's problems were found to be his parents' problems also: neither could be said to have had very good relationships with their own parents. On his sixth visit to the analyst it was found that when Kenneth's anger could be expressed, his wheezing could be stopped. In Kenneth can be seen a classic example of an over-controlled child whose ambivalent feelings are only to be expressed through his asthma. Nevertheless, under-control can be demonstrated to be an equally grave problem.

If most of the verbs in a paragraph are passive, as here, they take all the potential vigor and concision out of the sentences, making the most startling ideas sound tame. (Writing in the social sciences, as you can see above, succumbs especially to the passive epidemic.)

The solution is not to forbid you to use the passive, which can have special appropriateness when your idea is actually passive in sense. "The glory of the Lord shall be revealed" wonderfully suggests an unseen majestic actor. "It is said that. . ." can be viciously arch and ironic in the right context. And "Tax returns will be postmarked by midnight, 15 April" contains a threat from some hidden, abstract, and immovable authority. But these effects are special: they spring from situations where it is more powerful to conceal the real actor. Your rule should be this: *never use the passive voice unless you can tell yourself why*. The resulting victory for active verbs will of itself put muscle in your style.

Some other essential and ubiquitous verbs have even less action in them: "is" and the rest of the verb "to be," "seems," "becomes"—all of them denoting states of being. Much of the time we can't avoid them, but many writers use them unnecessarily when a more vigorous verb is crying out for the job. The only thing wrong with a sentence like

The federal government is very interested in speeding up urban redevelopment.

is that it lacks the conviction of

The federal government insists on speeding up urban redevelopment.

When you use "is," ask yourself if you aren't discriminating against a livelier verb that would energize your sentence.

The same applies to "there is" and "there are." Properly used, they denote existence as such ("There is a willow grows aslant a brook" or "There is a tide in the affairs of men / That taken at the flood leads on to fortune"). But don't use them as a stalling tactic at the beginning of a sentence while you puzzle out how to express it. Unnecessary verbs of being, like passives, force you into extended and clumsy sentence constructions and thus take the spring out of style. *Count the verbs in a page of your writing: if most of them are not vigorous active verbs, your ideas must sound impotent.*

Adjective Prostration and Overwriting.   You can induce this disease by generously coating your nouns with adjectives.

The arcaded brick-work, the fine, cut-stone quoins, and the elliptical fan-transoms mark out this charming old house as one of the most eclectic buildings in the gently hilly and sometimes rugged eastern part of this remarkably interesting, remote county.

In trying to crowd everything possible into this sentence, the writer has put at least one adjective in front of every noun. His attempt to define every substantive as precisely as possible is praiseworthy in the abstract, but the reader's ear grows weary of the relentless adjective-noun groups and the mind grows confused as to what the writer thinks most important. As with emphasis earlier, so with qualification here: if everything is modified, there is no discrimination, and the reader loses the thread that guides him through the sentence and the paragraph.

This state we may call *adjective prostration*; the reader, after a few mercilessly qualified sentences like the above, begins to breathe with difficulty. Two rules would help this writer. The first is to *use adjectives with restraint: don't qualify everything.* As an exercise you should write a page without using a single adjective or adverb. It can be done effectively and will show you that the strength of style is in those bones and sinews of the language—its nouns and its verbs. From these and little else, passage upon passage engrained in the English-speaking mind derives its effect.

The voice said, "Cry." And he said, "What shall I cry? All flesh is grass, and all the goodliness thereof is as the flower of the field. The grass withereth, the flower fadeth, because the spirit of the Lord bloweth upon it. Surely the people is grass. The grass withereth, the flower fadeth, but the word of our God shall stand forever."

—Isaiah, 40:6–8

I throw myself down in my chamber, and I call in and invite God and his angels thither. And when they are there, I neglect God and his angels for the noise of a fly, for the rattling of a coach, for the whining of a door.

—John Donne

Let us have faith that right makes might; and in that faith let us, to the end, dare to do our duty as we understand it.

—Abraham Lincoln

And so, my fellow Americans, ask not what your country can do for you—ask what you can do for your country.

—John F. Kennedy

The only notable adjectives above are "all" in the first quotation and "fellow" in the last.

Often a modest, ordinary adjective takes on unusual power in a context where adjectives are few. Notice the effectiveness of "true" and "all" in the following sentence by Jonathan Swift:

When a true genius appears in the world, you may know him by this sign, that the dunces are all in confederacy against him.

And in the following famous sentence from a speech made by Sir Winston Churchill during the Battle of Britain, the scarcity of adjectives throws weight on "finest":

Let us therefore brace ourselves to our duties, and so bear ourselves that, if the British Empire and its Commonwealth last for a thousand years, men will still say: "This was their finest hour."

Take this as a second rule: *state first, qualify afterwards.*

If you must qualify a lot, give the reader the simple form of the idea first; after that, you may qualify it, apply adjectives, and make finer distinctions in succeeding sentences. This strategy takes the psychology of the reader into account and will communicate with him better than sentences weighed down with adjectives. The tangled prose of

Now priceless, but undiscovered until 1947, the famous Dead Sea Scrolls, at first apparently only brittle parchment wrapped in foul-smelling rags, are celebrated as by far the most ancient known manuscripts of the Old Testament.

becomes more intelligible as a simple statement followed by the qualifications:

The Dead Sea Scrolls are celebrated as the most ancient manuscripts of the Old Testament. But, when discovered in 1947, these priceless documents appeared to be only brittle parchment wrapped in foul-smelling rags.

For corresponding overwriting with adverbs, the nickname *Tom Swifties* turns up, resurrected a few years ago in a parlor word-game. It came from a forgotten series of boys' books describing the exploits of a high-minded youth named, as you might suspect, Tom Swift. As his originator pictured him, Tom's clean living and social usefulness rested on a foundation of adverbs.

For Tom never just "said" anything: Tom said it "manfully." He never just "acted": he acted "decisively." The author's intentions may have been as pure as Tom's, but the rhetoric was naive and after a couple of pages, unintentionally funny. The point is not that adverbs are bad things, of course, but that they should not accompany every verb. Too often adverbs make verbs look crippled. Surely a good vigorous verb like "condemn" needs no crutch such as "roundly" or "forcibly." So *use adverbs with restraint to let the verbs sing out.*

Clichés and Other Weary Words.   Why, if you are convinced of something, must you be "firmly convinced"? Why shouldn't the "acid test" of "cherished beliefs" be an "outstanding record" (or in some cases, a "woeful lack") of "blissful ignorance"? How, when we have "forged ahead" with a "trusty guide" to "new heights" and "mountain-top experiences" in a "vast range" "ablaze with color" because "carpeted with flowers" and endured "sweeping changes" and even "winds of change" in the "climate of opinion" (supported, of course, on our "frames of reference"), will we still find strength to "explore every avenue," "strain every nerve," and "leave no stone unturned"?

These phrases are not news. Once they were, when they were first used. But since those long-ago coming-out parties they have become so familiar that we now use them and hundreds of other clichés and hackneyed combinations without really noticing their presence. That is what a cliché is: an expression that once was fresh but now scarcely registers. When you use an expression such as "blissful ignorance," it carries with it a staleness that gets through to the reader whether he consciously notices it as a cliché or not. Anyway, you probably mean only plain, unmodified "ignorance," which need not be "blissful" at all (the negative cliché is "painful ignorance"). If ignorance is what you mean, then "blissful ignorance," in addition to being stale, is misleading. These empty old phrases, when they occur in quantity, debase and cheapen the value of all words in the essay until it becomes hard for you to make the reader take any of your words precisely. Hence nuances of idea and verbal subtleties become impossible too.

In many political, government, and business statements, clichés are the basis (dare I say "stock-in-trade"?) of the necessary public statement that must be made but which should, according to function, say as little as possible. For example, see any statement released during a union-and-management dispute. In such a pronouncement, to "explore every avenue" can mean either that the negotiators will continue to try to find a compromise (the ordinary meaning of the cliché) or in fact that they have given up trying. That commentators must go to work figuring out what is meant indicates the effect clichés have on ordinary writing: they begin the sinister process of banishing meaning from words. So, *if you have heard a phrase before, look at it a second time. Does it say what you want to say? or is it simply a borrowed formula? If the latter, don't use it.* Make this a working rule.

Verbal Echo.   Here are two consecutive sentences from a book report Andy Adamson wrote in a political-science seminar:

Coleman's analysis of African political systems comes off somewhat better. As background Coleman sketches in the traditional culture and the patterns of Western impact.

The too-close repetition of "Coleman" suggests that Adamson has forgotten in the second sentence what he said in the first; otherwise his ear would have made him substitute "he" for the second "Coleman." No doubt he paused for a minute before writing the second sentence, and the sound of the first faded from his consciousness. He should have caught this lapse when he revised, however, for as they stand, the sentences, although connected in idea, sound as if they are falling apart.

This phenomenon I call *verbal echo.* Everybody perpetrates it now and then. When you do, there are three ways out. (1) Substitute a *pronoun* for the noun in the second reference, as in the example above. (2) If for the sake of clarity you must repeat a noun (suppose it is "analysis" in the example above), let the reader know that you know what you are doing by using a *demonstrative qualifier* like "this," "that," "such," "the same," and so on.

Coleman's *analysis* of African political systems comes off somewhat better. As background to *this analysis* he sketches in. . . .

(3) Substitute another *similar word,* maybe a synonym, in the second reference (a *Thesaurus* is invaluable here):

Coleman's *analysis* of African political systems comes off somewhat better. As background to the *investigation* he sketches in. . . .

This third method has an attendant vice, however, usually called *elegant variation.* To avoid repeating Shakespeare's name or substituting "he," would-be elegant writers try things like "the bard," "the Bard of Avon," "the Prince of Poets," or "the creator of *Hamlet.*" Even an ordinary cat may be subsequently denominated by "puss," "kitty," "feline," "feline predator," "mouser," "Tibbert," "Tabby," or for a really husky cat, "Leo." All this nonsense draws attention to the very act of avoiding echo. Thus elegant variation is not elegant at all but clumsy and heavy-handed. By making its author sound like a fool, it is, as a cure for echo, much worse than the disease.

Sometimes when you use pronouns to avoid echo you will find yourself juggling more than one at a time so that they become ambiguous:

Almond sets up functional economic categories as the basis for investigation, and his co-author Coleman applies them to forty-six African countries. But when he. . . .

Who is "he" here? Almond or Coleman? Andy Adamson saw the problem coming and thought that he had solved it by this clumsy stratagem:

But when he (Coleman). . . .

Never do this. Although you will sometimes find it in print, the pronoun-with-parenthesis-explanation always contains an embarrassing admission that you can't manage your own sentence. What Adamson should have done is to repeat the name, echo or not.

But when Coleman. . . .

There is no other way here to be understood.

How Many Words? The prolix and expansive prose of the nineteenth century implied readers with some leisure as well as a taste for the elaborate. Modern prose tends to be concise, spare, and rapid-moving. This conciseness makes for efficient reading, of course, and is consistent with the contemporary taste for the clean, trim, and functional. In other words, conciseness and economy of style is now an ideal in writing.

Practically, this means that *you should use no more words than will get your whole meaning across.* If the reader senses superfluity in your style, he will begin to skim and thus slip beyond your control, taking whatever his eye happens to light on as the cruxes of your argument. On the other hand, if he finds your style compact or even dense, he can always read more slowly. You should be reasonable about compactness, however: if you are too sparing of words, your prose will be simply cryptic and puzzling. We have all read paragraphs where a few more words or a couple of extra sentences would make all the difference between clarity and obscurity.

Writing in the social sciences is a special stronghold of wordiness (although some writing in the humanities can scarcely be called terse). Educationists and sociologists are the legendary offenders. Lately the sociologists have begun to reform their prose and to make it cleaner, more concise, and more human, but that reform did not quite get through to the following statement, an astonishing example of how wordy even a short sentence can be:

In general, Cleveland married couples may be safely said to engage in a considerable amount and variety of joint activity both inside and outside the home.

So many words say so little here that at first I suspected that there was no intelligible meaning at all. What is really being said, I now think, is that "Married couples in Cleveland do a lot of things together"—a rather modest revelation to take up twenty-six words. If this is what the writer meant, however, why didn't he put it so concisely in the first place?

Verbosity is still worse in a long sentence than in a short one. In the following quotation the writer falls incestuously so in love with his words that he begets a no-language called *gobbledygook*:

Although it is suggested that certain of these methods are more justified under certain conditions and for the investigation of certain problems than for other conditions and problems, conformity to the specified measurement and sampling requirements will, in the final analysis, offer the only assurance of validity.

This is the kind of thing a computer might say to itself in the middle of the night. It is not English but a solemn fraud. When you try to translate it into meaning, you find that it does not of itself make sense: "Although some of these methods will sometimes work, following the rules given will assure validity." What does this mean? Apparently the writer intends to say this: "Although the recommended methods may not work in every case, you will do well in the long run to follow them." If this is his meaning, he has lost control over it by using so many words. "I wish he would explain his explanation," says Lord Byron in another context.

You are your style

"Style," says H. L. Mencken, "is always the outward and visible sign of a man, and it cannot be anything else." The essence of style is you—your individuality, your particular voice, your unique way of thinking and speaking. But this cannot be taught. For better or worse, it is you, and you are it. If your writing were entirely you, however, the rest of us could not understand it, just as we could not understand the private hodgepodge of short-cut logic, associations, and formulas you use in thinking or talking to yourself. If writing is to communicate (and that is its only legitimate aim), then it must express your own particular voice according to the standards and forms (such as sentences, paragraphs, arrangement, etc.) accepted by all readers. Explaining these has been my business from Chapter Two to this point. *The whole strategy of good style is this: to fulfill these standards while making your own voice heard.* If you don't fulfill the standards and write by the rules, you certainly won't control your reader's comprehension. But if you don't allow your own voice to come through, you may be clear but not worth reading.

The Cult of Mere Correctness. There are two things wrong with the style of much undergraduate writing: its willingness to be merely correct and its excessive formality. Both spell death to the writer's own voice. To deal with mere correctness first. You must not imagine that faithful observation of all the rules in this book will give your writing style. Instead they are part of your technical equipment as a writer, equipment indispensable for communication. By themselves, however, they cannot make your unique personality find its "outward and visible sign" in the black-and-white of the page. Sound rules, impeccable grammar, meticulous spelling—if your writing aims to achieve no more than these, then it will, even when you succeed, only enroll you in the colorless ranks of Natural C. Plus and Lucky Breaks.

One of my reasons for introducing Andy Adamson and Basil Richards into this book is to underscore their difference. This difference begins with each man's uniqueness as a person. Each thinks differently, reacts differently, speaks differently. Why shouldn't this difference color his writing? It does. Adamson eventually learns the rules, Richards reluctantly agrees to operate by them. But when each becomes an effective writer, it is in his own way: Adamson on the Inner City does not sound at all like Richards on the churches of Italy. The rules give form and efficiency to the communication, but the voice communicating remains distinctly individual. If there were a master rule about style it would be this: *sound like yourself*; let your own voice and personality come through.

What you say in a paper necessarily has much to do with how you yourself have come to see the subject. For the paper almost unavoidably expresses not the standard view but your own view of the evidence, your own ordering of material, your own impression of what is important and secondary and trivial. So you shouldn't be at all backward about making your presence felt. Don't be afraid to say "I think," "I find," "It seems to me," "Let me first," and so on. I am not arguing for a cheek-to-cheek approach. Don't make the reader feel that you are settling your hand on his knee. But let him know that he is reading a communication put together and controlled not by a data-processing machine but by the intelligence and imagination of someone warm, breathing, thinking, and intellectually alive. Reading such writing is like reading the person. When this happens to well-ordered prose, it has style.

The Cult of Formality.   Although we live in an age increasingly informal in every way, too many undergraduates labor under the impression that their writing should sound as formal as possible. If it must be formal, then writing cannot be much like the probably informal writer who writes it, and hence it will be nearly impossible for him to let his voice come through. Once I taught a lively and attractive girl who in no way lacked distinguishing qualities. Yet in an early freshman paper she wrote a sentence beginning "One is interested *of* this for the reason that." Of course she would have said in any other context, "I am interested *in* this because," or (better) "My interest *in* this comes from." But her effort was to make the paper sound as formal as possible, and she went about it by expunging every human touch, producing a chilly, wasteful sentence capped with "interested of." When I asked her about this novel contribution to the development of the language, she admitted, after thinking a bit, that she always said "interested in," had never heard "interested of" used before, and had probably coined this idiom because "it somehow sounded more formal." In fact, it doesn't sound more formal; it sounds bizarre, an English equivalent to Fractured French. If this freshman had written as she spoke when speaking carefully, her paper would have had a chance at style. For ordinarily, *good student writing is informal in tone like good speech*. It differs from speech mainly by being much more condensed, better organized, and less wasteful.

Not surprisingly, it is the inexperienced writer who feels that writing must be vastly more formal than good speech and that he must fracture every idiom to make it so. The linguistic distortions and grotesqueries that pockmark freshman and other college papers, and which instructors usually annotate helplessly as "awkward" or "not English" because there is no way of dealing with them, commonly originate from this misguided quest for formality. Furthermore, these absurdities of idiom make it clear that the devotees of Formality worship from afar in solemn ignorance, without having any idea of what real formality is.

Problems in decorum

There are certain writing situations that demand a formal treatment. Adjusting your style to audience and subject in such cases was anciently labeled *decorum*, which Milton called "the

grand masterpiece to observe." (Because no more inclusive name
for the process has ever appeared, it seems worthwhile to restore
the old term.) If you think how differently you would write a
letter to an intimate friend and a letter to a college dean, then
you will see that decorum is socially instinctive and that you
have known something about it all along. Sometimes you may
find it necessary to write in a more formal manner than you are
used to, because the subject or the occasion (e.g., an occasion of
sorrow affecting someone you do not know well) or maybe the
tastes of a particular instructor require it. To distinguish the
formal and informal in such cases, consider three criteria: the
contraction of verbs, the manner in which you wish to represent
yourself and address your reader, and the level of diction.

1. Using Contractions. The liberties the writer takes with
verb contractions usually give away at once the level of formality
at which he conceives himself to be writing. Is it "isn't" or "is
not," "wouldn't" or "would not"? Of course "isn't" is typical of
speech and thus informal. Some instructors can't stand it and
other contractions in any context. So be warned. I think it perfectly natural but much too easygoing for a formal situation.
Oddly enough, while the negative contractions sound fine in informal writing, the positive contractions such as "I'll," "I'm,"
"it's," "we'd," and "they'd" do not, unless the manner you are
using is very informal indeed. Many instructors would accept
"it's," "I'm," and "you're" if the paper were uniformly informal
in tone, but not the *will-* or *would-* contractions such as "I'll"
and "they'd," which to most readers sound too colloquial for
expository writing and a little sloppy, as if you had egg on your
face. There is no permanently valid reason for this. We simply
are here confronting usage—what is usually done in certain
situations and what is not.

2. Representing Yourself and Addressing Your Reader. The
informal manner inclines toward conversation, the formal to
proclamation—or at least these are the extremes. How should you
appear? as relaxed or rigid? as conversing or anonymously pro-
claiming? Would you say "I think" or "one thinks"? This is the
key. A few instructors (usually those who don't like "isn't") insist
on the anonymous formality of "one," but it seems schoolmarm-

ish to me unless by it you mean yourself as representing what should be everybody's opinion (e.g., "One cannot contemplate genocide with less than revulsion"). In this sense of "everybody" or "many," "one" is invaluable. In any but an emphatically formal context, however, the use of "one" for ordinary, personal "I" makes the student writer sound like a nineteen-year-old oracle.

How you address your reader is a related problem in decorum. It once was the practice, when an author acknowledged the existence of his reader, to address him indirectly and categorically as "the reader" ("The reader can doubtless furnish instances from his own experience"). This stiffly conventional habit is practiced now only in severely formal writing, perhaps because it seems insulting to reduce a flesh-and-blood reader to an abstraction. He is, after all, an individual reader, not any reader. In anything less than the most formal writing, most writers now admit that their book may be open and some living person reading it and thus address him directly as "you" ("You can no doubt supply examples from your own experience"). Once again, the effect is to bridge the gap between writer and reader, making the ideas expressed seem more immediate.

3. *Choosing a Level of Diction.*   Most commonly used words have no sense of level attached to them. "Is," "because," "finds," "person," "behavior": no one can speak without using such words. But sometimes there are choices. Is it to be "go" or "proceed," "deep" or "profound," "outline" or "adumbrate," "show" or "evince," "howling" or "ululation"? Each pair consists of what Fowler calls an outdoor word and an indoor word. Obviously "evince" is less common than "show" and would be considered more formal. I do not mean that every word in formal writing should be of the rarity of "adumbrate" or "ululation" but rather that the proportion of such words will be higher. You would not likely use many such words unless you considered your essay's style formal. When you aren't compelled to adopt a formal style, stick to the simpler, or outdoor, word unless an indoor word, with its special connotations, happens to say exactly what you mean.

The outdoor and indoor words above have one quality in

common: they are literate. No one would blanch to find them in writing. Because no dictionary labels them, it implies that they are *standard* and to be used without fear of impropriety. Most English words, from "cat" to "catachresis," are standard in this sense. But there are some labels used by dictionaries to indicate that certain words are not standard and hence not normally to be used in writing. *Archaic* is the label for linguistic antiques —words still understood but read only in older literature: "anent," "aplenty," "aught," "perchance," "raiment," "yore," "whit." Never use these stained-glass words even though you have seen them in print. The classical translations of the Bible (King James and Douay) are full of them, but in contemporary writing they sound pompous and absurd. The label *substandard* usually includes particularly colloquial words and slang. *Colloquial* means that a word is proper in casual speech but exceptional in writing: "blue" (sad), "enthuse," "flake out," "high" (drunk), "jam" (predicament), "kids," "like" (as conjunction), "pinch" (steal), "phony," "squeal" (betray). *Slang*, of course, is even lower on the scale and proper only in the most easy-going speech: "ace" (succeed in), "cool," "corny," "fink," "goof," "goofball," "lousy," "rat" (betray), "ratfink."

Slang and colloquial words are like hot air in a special sense: they tend to rise. The few slang words that become established often ascend to colloquial status (are "ace" and "lousy" already colloquial?); and some colloquial words tend eventually to find their way into good writing. The escalation of words is part of the dynamics of linguistic development, but it is a dangerous process for a writer to anticipate. Ordinarily, it is safe to use a colloquial or slang word in your writing only when you see it frequently in the work of serious, experienced writers. You can, of course, always check in a good up-to-date dictionary to see whether the word in question is labeled "slang" or "colloquial." But dictionaries inevitably lag somewhat behind usage, so the practice of good contemporary writers is a better guide. An even better guide, and the ultimate one, is your own fallible common sense.

For there are very few linguistic absolutes. Most people who write or teach or read or care about language imagine that there are, because most of us want to make our own verbal habits absolute and mandatory for everyone else. The man who invariably and conscientiously uses "shall" in the first person, "will" in the second, and reverses them for emphasis, is scandalized by writers who ignore this distinction. To me the distinction is completely artificial, but to say so is no doubt part of my own linguistic absolutism. Fowler's *Modern English Usage* (recommended earlier in this chapter) offers a clear example of this absolutism. When Fowler places a word according to absolute categories of correctness (and incorrectness), not every literate person will accept his decision. What *Modern English Usage* really presents is a compendium of one man's inevitably absolute opinions on points of usage. Because that man is clearheaded, precise, learned, and intelligent, it is invaluable to have his opinions at your finger tips as a guide. But they are nevertheless opinions about what Fowler conceives to be normal usage.

An amusing demonstration that we all want to turn our own linguistic habits into absolutes occurred in 1961 when Merriam-Webster published the third edition of the standard reference dictionary of American libraries, *Webster's New International Dictionary (Unabridged)*. This 13½-pound tome broke through a strange frontier by largely abandoning the expected labeling system for words: colloquial, slang, erroneous, etc. The editors were following a respectable theory in modern linguistics that attempts to describe the language objectively and scientifically rather than to exercise authority over its usage and prescribe what is to be correct and incorrect. But they didn't get away scot-free. In fact, the outraged complaints of reviewers, readers, and other literate people who have always expected a reference dictionary to provide some label of usage and relative correctness have hardly yet died away. In a practical sense they are right. For it is more helpful to read Fowler and disagree with his opinion than to look up a word in *Webster's Third* and find there (usually) no indication of what the editors regard, admittedly from their own absolute points of view, as acceptable or unacceptable written usage.

What does all this mean to you when you have to choose appropriate words? Simply this: you are inevitably your own linguistic absolutist. So you must make your own choices, using as much common sense, experience, and taste as you can muster. Obviously you should stick to acceptable standard words and among them choose only the words that say precisely what you mean. This is not always, or often, the word that comes first to your mind. But sometimes the precise word may happen to be colloquial ("phony") or even slang ("goof"). What should you do then? If you really believe the word says what you mean, go ahead and use it, as Andy Adamson does in the first sentence quoted from his Inner-City paper: "The hayseed, then, used to be considered a poor country cousin of the city slicker. . . ." But don't put *apologetic quotation marks* around a substandard word ("hayseed," "city slicker") to show that you know you are slumming: that only shows insecurity. If you must use it because it is the precise word for the job, then use it without apology and take full responsibility. It is decidedly unwise, however, to use substandard words readily or indiscriminately in papers. Students who write "When Laertes hits the scene back at Elsinore, Hamlet treats him like the fink he is" are in danger of leaving school precipitately.

Finding a Style. These three then—the use of verb contractions, the way you represent yourself and address your reader, and the choice of a level of diction—are the chief devices governing relative formality of style (not "interest of" and other abnormalities). The main problem is to find a style appropriate to you—your gifts, your way of thinking, your own degree of formality. For most undergraduates in most situations it will be useful if you *make a literate, precise, but informal style your ordinary style.* (The middle style might be a better term.) From the three criteria above you can see what its hallmarks will be:

1. the negative contractions will be permissible;
2. the author will be "I," the reader "you"; and
3. words will be mainly of the simple, outdoor variety (indoor and occasionally even substandard words will occur when they alone achieve the effect you want).

I recommend this level of style because it seems congenial to the writing temperament of many undergraduates and is the style used more and more by professional writers. (It is, incidentally, the style I have kept to in writing this book.) Furthermore, it is the most convenient level of style from which to move up to formality or down to more informality, according to the demands of decorum. By manipulating the three criteria above, you can easily raise your style a notch or two when occasion requires it: the contractions will disappear; the author will step back a little and be less familiar (he should still be "I," however, but a less frequently present "I"); and the proportion of indoor words may increase a little, with all substandard words definitely forbidden. But the literate, informal style will generally serve you better, by permitting your own voice and presence to come through—which is nearly impossible when an undergraduate gropes for a formal manner. For this reason I insist on a literate but informal style in most of my students' papers. One other reason is that it is too easy to write formally and write badly (see the examples of professional sociological writing quoted earlier in this chapter). Professional academic journals, traditional strongholds of formal writing, can seldom be cited for their excellence of style. In fact, many of their severely formal articles sound inane. If mature writers don't succeed in making the formal manner fresh and engaging (it can be), then you should stick to the informal.

Above all, when choices of words, and style generally, confront you, *choose what sounds most natural to you.* That will reflect you more, including your own tendency to be absolute about words, for that is part of your individuality too. In the long run, choosing what you think sounds natural will contribute more to style than choosing what you think you are expected to choose. A distinguished senior colleague recently made a remark to me about student papers that, if I may paraphrase him, went something like this: "I can forgive an undergraduate a lot of technical writing errors, if in his paper he sounds like himself and I can hear a real intelligence that doesn't merely ape all the other men in the class." More and more readers of papers would agree.

Points to remember

1. Use a new word in writing only when you have learned it in context and checked its meaning in a good up-to-date dictionary.
2. Have Fowler's *Modern English Usage* and Roget's *Thesaurus* handy.
3. Never use the passive voice unless you can tell yourself why.
4. Use vigorous active verbs whenever you can.
5. Use adjectives and adverbs with restraint. Don't try to qualify everything.
6. State first, qualify afterwards.
7. Never use a cliché unless it says precisely what you mean.
8. Avoid verbal echo.
9. Use no more words than will get your whole meaning across.
10. Above all, sound like yourself.
11. Whenever possible, make the informal level your ordinary level of style.

Revision: where good papers are made

CHAPTER NINE

"That's not writing, that's typing," Truman Capote is supposed to have said when told of a writer who boasted of never revising. This suggests the importance of revision, so great that I cannot stress it too much. Although there are only a few things to know about it, revision makes all the difference between good writing and bad writing. Yet many students toss it off as inconsequential—a nuisance once the paper is written. But of course the paper really isn't written at all until you have revised it. Unrevised, it is only a draft; and a draft isn't a paper. Nor is it doing enough to flip through, checking for sense and obvious errors: this isn't revising. Real revision requires that you switch roles: you stop being the creator of the paper and become its critic. When you revise adequately, you get the first crack at judging your own paper and thus can prepare the defenses against later criticisms from your reader. Even more important, you get a chance to see what your best ideas and effects are and to revise and rearrange so that they get the prominence they deserve. Revision is, above all, your chance to put your best foot forward.

But before you revise

Leave Space in Your Draft for Revision. A colleague of mine in engineering who types his first draft always triple-spaces the lines so that when he revises he has room to change every sentence at least twice. Other writers who do their drafts by hand use only every second or third line. The point of this technique, of course, is that a first draft with regular, open spaces is maximally flexible and takes much of the awkwardness out of revision. In his book *Style*, F. L. Lucas suggests that besides writing on widely spaced lines, it is useful to write on only one-third or one-quarter of the page. Alexander Pope worked out his poems down the left-hand half of a ledger page, then used the other half in revising. Extra space is invaluable when you find that alteration of words and individual sentences is not enough and that you must rewrite whole passages or add extensive new material. If you do a proper job of invention and disposition before you begin to write the draft, however, you will seldom find that you need to rewrite the whole thing. Once you have a completed draft, stick with it as your basic text and revise it but don't rewrite. Sometimes a student comes in with two versions of his paper saying "I wasn't satisfied with the first version so I sat down and wrote another. Now I can't decide which is better." Usually both are of the same quality. This student would have been much better off had he concentrated on improving and polishing his original draft.

The Fallow Period. Although I said it before in Chapter Two, I must insist on the point once again here: you cannot criticize your rough draft just after you have finished it. You are too flushed with composition, too close to what you have just written, too involved to take an objective view. At this point it is your brain child, and if anyone else gave so much as a hint of attacking or even questioning it, you would behave like a she-bear with cubs. When you have finished the draft of a paper, put it away immediately. Don't reread it, don't tinker with it, don't take a miles-to-go-before-I-sleep attitude toward it. Go to a movie, do your physics or French, decline into a coma if you like. But don't touch your finished draft. The longer you can keep it locked up the better, but *put it away for at least twenty-four hours.* During that fallow period banish it from your mind entirely. When later you come back and pull it out of refrigeration you will be amazed that it seems almost like someone else's work. Now that you can read it objectively, you are ready to turn it into the good paper it potentially is. Of course, being able to find a fallow period depends on your personal organization. If you wrote the draft in a forty-eight hour crisis, as Mike Harris did, then you might as well forget about revision altogether. Any revision you attempt then could not possibly be objective: you might destroy the best things you have done.

How Much Revision? This depends on how you wrote the draft. In the matter of drafts there are two kinds of people. Some, probably the majority, write theirs straightforwardly, pausing as little as possible to make changes, hoping only to get down a completed rough text. If you have the temperament for it, this is the more efficient way, but obviously it means that revision will be extremely important and will entail a lot of work. The old principle "Write in haste and revise at leisure" will apply especially to you. Some less fortunate people, like me, can't bear to write a draft without fiddling, crossing out, correcting, and rephrasing while they write. This is not efficient and produces a palimpsest-like manuscript that makes sense only to the writer and his mother. But when they begin to revise, they have much less to do. Nevertheless, both kinds of writers must go through the same series of steps when they revise. No one, no matter how he does his rough draft, can know in advance what booby traps and land mines he has implanted in it unawares.

Trouble Spots to Expect. As you take up your now cooled-off rough draft, brace yourself for a possible shock, for you may find the beginning something of a disappointment, much worse than you had imagined. Don't let this depress you, for *the worst writing usually comes at the beginning of a paper.* This means, of course, that in revising you should be especially critical of the first few paragraphs, for when you wrote them you were also in the throes of getting a feeling for that paper. (If by the time you have read through the first third of the draft, you still find it riddled with errors, inconsistencies, and infelicities, then prepare for the worst. Maybe it is genuinely bad throughout and you will have a long, hard night ahead of you.) The other place to look for special difficulties is at *any section that you remember writing while tired or bored,* especially the section just before the end. When the writer's energy slackens and he begins to write mechanically from his notes, then anything can happen, but the chances of its being good are slim.

How to revise

Revision, to be efficient and effective, must be orderly. It is not enough simply to read through your draft looking for what you might like to change. The following four steps are essential for profitable revision:

1. Cut Away the Fat.   We all use words too freely: they should be rationed. Most of our first drafts are like ballplayers after a winter of TV, beer, and pretzels: to get them lean, solid, and in condition, we must trim them down. Nobody has put this more sharply than the early-nineteenth-century writer and wit, Sydney Smith: "In composition, as a general rule, run your pen through every other word you have written; you have no idea what vigor it will give to your style." And so you should. *Cross out every needless word, sentence, maybe even paragraph.* Go through your whole draft doing this first, because there is no point in revising the least jot or tittle if you later cross it out. As you excise, many problems of future revision will evaporate. Look especially at the first few paragraphs or even pages. Not only does the beginning often display the worst writing, but it is often a relic of the writing process, useful in warming you up to the first draft but now past that usefulness. Or it may turn out to be the irrelevant introduction described in Chapter Six. Or its material may now appear trivial and far from the heart of the subject. So consider whether you can cut a whole slice away from the beginning. Many papers would have seized the reader's attention at once had they begun a page or two later.

When cutting, the handiest tool you can own is some brand of black *wide felt-tipped pen.* A felt pen blacks out words and lines so absolutely that not a shred remains to distract your eyes as you read. If you can still manage to read a word crossed out scratchily by pen or pencil, you can't get an accurate idea of what the passage is like without it.

2. Read Aloud for Content.   When it comes to *detecting errors, the ear is twice as efficient as the eye.* So read your trimmed-down draft aloud slowly, *listening to the sense.* After the fallow period and the cutting, it should sound alien enough for you to ask honest, critical questions: "Is the main point of this paragraph clear?" "How did I get to this idea? Is something really confused? Or is it just a matter of a missing transition or an explicit connective?" "Haven't I said this before? So why slug it home again here?" "Can I add anything to make this paragraph sharper? Is its progress logical? Can I simplify it? Do I need an illustration or more detail to make the point solid?" You should try to ask questions like these after you read each paragraph. If they are relevant, then something needs sharpening or rewriting. If they aren't, then either the paragraph is clear and controlled or you should turn up your hearing aid. Whenever a question about clarity or meaning arises, set to work at once to *simplify*. Confusion nearly always coincides with unnecessary complexity (provided, of course, that you weren't truly confused when you wrote). When something seems unclear, ask yourself "What do I really mean here?" As you answer, you will simultaneously simplify, clarify, and revise the problem passage.

At the end of the first reading aloud, ask yourself if the basic points of the disposition or outline are unmistakable and emphatic. Test this, if you have a long-suffering roommate, by reading the draft to him, then *giving him an unannounced quiz*, something like this: "Summarize this paper in three statements" or "What are the main points made here?" (What you were attempting to say will, of course, determine the form of this quiz.) If your roommate failed to pick up your main points or you find yourself saying "What I meant was. . . ," something is terribly amiss. You had better go through the draft again, simplifying and emphasizing the main ideas.

3. Read Aloud for Style.   When you have repaired your argument to insure sense and clarity, read the draft through aloud once more, *listening to the rhythm*. Keep your ears pricked for the sedative and washboard effects, verbal echoes, adjective prostration, and the other problems of style discussed in Chapters Seven and Eight.

You should be warned that *cutting and revising may have given rise to difficulties of style that were not there before*. For instance, cutting may have produced a series of similar or short sentences, a problem easily remedied if you let your ear pick it out for you. Or in revising the content you may have rammed rhythmically incompatible sentences into one; your ear will tell you, to borrow the Ogden Nash quip, that "you can't get there from here" and had better make two sentences. Or in cutting and condensing you may have poured too much into a single sentence by adding dependent clauses everywhere. I did just this many times in revising a draft of my M.A. thesis. By using "which" clauses recklessly to make each sentence carry an enormous freight of meaning, I had made the reader gulp and strain in his effort to follow what I said. After a few pages of this, the ordinarily temperate director of my thesis found himself abused beyond endurance. He took revenge by writing "WHICH" over and over again from top to bottom down the margin of a page. I got the unsubtle message and have never since used "which" without a pang. At this stage, then, *listen for the too complex as well as the tediously simple.*

Finally, keep one ear cocked for the pretentious, the pompous, the formal—anything that doesn't sound like you. A sophomore in one of my classes just lately wrote a sentence beginning "I have this perspicacity into. . . ." It was his little offering to the Cult of Formality, for ordinarily he would say "I see." As he revised, his ear should have picked up this distorted, unidiomatic, and unnaturally pompous expression—a kind of parody of formal writing. In fact, there is a queer-sounding, traditional rule, never seen in any textbook but handed down by word of mouth through generations of students and instructors: *if you like it, cross it out.* It is not quite so startling as it sounds, however. It refers to passages, sentences, or even phrases where the writer has tried to create a showy or flashy effect and has succeeded instead in producing a bit of self-conscious, flowery, contrived prose—too extravagant for its context and sticking out from the page as if written in red. You can always detect such a passage when revising, because the moment you come to it, you will recall the contortions you went through to compose it and will feel uneasily proud. That is the time to cross it out. "Naturalness," says Anatole France, "is what is added last."

4. Don't Forget Your Errors List. By now you are a full-fledged critic. Although your original draft has taken a beating, it should be a much better example of your writing. Your best ideas and your own original approach should now be shining through. But remember this: in previous papers that you thought finished enough to hand in, instructors still found errors to red-pencil. What makes you sure you have not made them again in this final draft? After all, your previous convictions are on record and your criminal tendencies are known. As a final step, then, take out your duly compiled and cumulative Errors List, note the faults memorialized there (if you really want to write well, you will know them by heart), and then read your final draft through slowly, not aloud this time, looking for those specific sins. You will likely find that in spite of all this revision you have overlooked a couple of the same errors. Once you catch them, your improvement is guaranteed. If at this stage you abandon the Errors-List procedure, however, errors are prone to become more entrenched and thus a permanent disability in your style. You can only beat a habitual error for good by consciously establishing the contrary habit.

And last, copyread

Now you are ready to type the final copy. If you don't type, learn to; in the meantime have your papers typed. A typed paper is always more convincing than one written by hand and, I am afraid, always worth a few extra points. Perhaps this should not happen, but it does and will continue to as long as readers are human and live in something less than the best of all possible worlds. Next to suicide, the most grievous sin you can commit is to blame errors in your paper on a typist. Shockingly often, a student tells me, "I was too busy to type this so my roommate did it for me and he made a lot of mistakes." There must be some special palm-fringed corner of heaven, with dancing girls and white-sand beaches, set aside for just such saintly and sinned-against typists.

A Carbon Copy Is Insurance. When you type a fair copy, always make a carbon copy as well and keep it until you get the graded paper back. Papers can get lost, stolen, or destroyed. More than a few have simply evaporated, to the embarrassment of both student and instructor. When this happens, no matter who is to blame, the writer who can't produce a carbon copy is like an uninsured homeowner surveying the smouldering ruins. Considering how little trouble it is to make, a carbon gives you protection of the most cut-rate kind imaginable.

Copyread Twice. Copyreading (sometimes called proofreading) is your responsibility, not your typist's. To do it right you must *read through the typed copy twice*: (1) for sense, to make sure that nothing—a phrase, a sentence, often a line or even a passage—has been left out; and (2) for accuracy of words. Ignoring the sense, look carefully at each word to see that it is spelled right and that letters in it have not been transposed. Remember, once you hand in a paper there is no such thing as a typo: it is an error, chargeable to you. When an error involves only a few words, most instructors would be content if it were erased and corrected neatly in ink.

Careful revision is your insurance that the effort you put into invention, disposition, and expression will show to advantage when your paper is read. When you complete this final step, you can look back over the process of writing the paper and know that it is the product of orderly method. Further, you will realize that this method has given you more control over the writing process than you ever had before. When you augment it with a personal Errors List to make criticism of your writing pay, you have guaranteed your improvement in writing from paper to paper. To apply these techniques, now that you know them, is only common sense. To ignore them is to slip back into the hopeless and overcrowded underworld where we found Natural C. Plus and Lucky Breaks.

Points to remember

1. Leave space in your first draft for lots of revising.
2. Don't attempt to revise for at least twenty-four hours after you have written the first draft.
3. Expect the worst writing to come at the beginning of your draft and also in any section you wrote while bored or tired.
4. The first act of revision is to cut out everything you can.
5. The second is to read aloud for content.
6. The third is to read aloud once more for style.
7. Check your revised draft against your Errors List.
8. Copyread twice, once for sense and once for individual words.

Key to the Errors Lists
of chapter one

In their first six weeks of using the Errors-List technique, Andy Adamson and Basil Richards managed to record, between them, some of the most typical and frequent errors in undergraduate writing. Because their abilities and backgrounds were so different, their combined lists give a broad coverage to these difficulties. In the alphabetical entries below I have either explained each of their errors and shown how to avoid it, or if it has been treated elsewhere in this book, I have indicated where the discussion of it may be found. Entries are listed by the key word; for example, "dangling participle" is listed as "participle, dangling."

"**and/or.**" This clumsy and unpleasant device is fortunately never necessary. The writer needs only "or." If

French 15 and/or French 20 is required for entrance to the major. . . ,

then anyone who has French 15 *or* French 20 will be admitted. Anyone who has both simply has more than the minimum requirements. If you see some special reason for writing "and/or," write instead "French 15 or French 20 or both." This is a little longer but avoids barbarity.

anticlimax in organization. Whether you end with a special final paragraph or not (see *valid final paragraphs*, pp. 85–89), make sure you end with a good firm point. Anticlimax occurs when the writer has obviously finished his paper, then thinks of a minor point or qualification or bit of detail—anything not centrally important to the argument of the paper—and sticks it on at the end.

"**as.**" This is inelegant used causally. When "as" means "because" and occurs late in the sentence, it sounds unpleasant:

We went home, as it was late.

Most readers would accept

As it was late, we went home.

But in either case there is no need for "as," which is used much too freely in bad writing, has the other and more essential meaning of "while" or "during," and can always be profitably replaced by "because," which has only one meaning. So when "as" means "because," always use "because."

clichés. See *clichés and other weary words*, pp. 116–17.

conclusion, unjustified. See *final paragraph*, pp. 85–89, especially *do you need a special final paragraph?* p. 85, and *proof established*, pp. 86–87.

copyread. See *and last, copyread*, pp. 136–37.

detail, excessive. See also *illustrate* and *generalization*, both below. Occasionally a paper suffocates in detail, although more often it expires in the oxygen-poor air of generalization. The right amount of detail is the amount that particularizes the point, that roots an air-borne generalization in solid ground. To say

Hemingway became a disappointing writer as he grew older.

is mere unconvincing opinion. But if you can add details, like

In late novels like *The Old Man and the Sea*, for instance, he substitutes telling for showing, in an attempt to make us feel heroism and pathos through rhetoric and not through spectacle. The image of the disciplined contest against nature, basic to the early works, has become blurred.

then the generalization begins to have body. But remember that enough is enough. If details proliferate unnecessarily, the reader may lose contact with the larger idea they embody.

digressions. When you have developed a flexible outline (see *a more flexible technique for disposition*, pp. 46–48), you should stick to it. When you feel an urge to digress into material not on your outline, ask yourself if it is a true digression or new and relevant information. If the latter, rearrange your outline to accommodate it. See *the outline as catalyst*, pp. 60–61.

exclamation points for emphasis. The writer who uses this mechanical form of emphasis readily soon finds himself doubling and even tripling it to indicate degrees of emphasis.

Raskolnikov finds himself trapped! At the top of the stairs he sees Porfiry Petrovich, the image of the law, but at the bottom he sees Sonia, the image of his conscience!!!

This writer is using exclamation points to bludgeon ordinary sentences into inarticulate pulp. The exclamation point is seldom necessary in expository writing (its main use is in fictional dialogue). Use it only when your statement is truly remarkable. Otherwise, the exclamation point will suggest that you can't manage the words of your sentence to achieve proper emphasis. See *common sense about emphasis*, pp. 105–7.

"Firstly." See p. 49.

generalization, too much. See *detail* above, and *illustrate* below. The ideal in writing is a balance of general statement against detail or illustration. An excess of generalization quickly renders the reader's mind blank. Statements like

There are some activities of thought that prepare the mind for ultimate engagement

should not predominate in your writing lest your reader's mind become as transparent as glass and no more retentive. Too much generalization means that he will begin to pay less and less attention and so miss your real meaning.

illustrate, failure to. The well-known Chinese saying that a picture is worth a thousand words applies neatly to writing. Say it, then let us see it: keep this principle in mind as you compose. Some of us find it much too easy to deal in abstractions and generalizations that seem clear to us. But if you put yourself in the reader's place, as you should when you write and especially when you revise, you will begin to appreciate the Chinese saying. If one illustration clarifies the point, however, that is enough and better than three poor or tangential illustrations.

inflated and repetitious. See *how many words?* pp. 118–20, and *cut away the fat*, p. 153.

inversions of subject and verb. A mannerism is any device correct in itself but that, when used commonly, becomes a prominent feature of your style and hence tedious. Inversions of subject and verb, rhetorical questions, and frequent repetition of a conspicuous and unusual word ("plethora" for "variety" or "cogitate" for "think") are typical mannerisms.

Inversion of the normal order of subject and verb is a particularly pompous, useless, and surprisingly common mannerism in undergraduate writing. It occurs frequently in older poetry and in the prose of the Bible:

Male and female created He them.
The horse and his rider hath He thrown into the sea.
In the beginning was the Word.

But in ordinary prose its poetic quality usually makes the writer sound as if he were striving self-consciously for an odd effect. It usually occurs toward the end of a paper when the writer feels a need to wax eloquent.

That so must we do is imperative.
At this point returns Achilles to his tents.

This mannerism serves a purpose in only one case, when the inversion of the verb or its auxiliary allows an adverb to be thrown emphatically toward the beginning of the sentence:

Suddenly down came the hail.
Even less did he like the grinding sounds from the transmission.
Slow, much too slow are the judgments of God.

Otherwise, avoid it.

italics (underlining) for emphasis. See *underlining for emphasis,* below.

"like": not a conjunction. Although almost universal in informal American speech and reinforced by the inescapable advertisement ("like a cigarette should"), "like" cannot introduce clauses in good written English. Someday it no doubt will, but the obvious incongruity of "like" in the following sentence shows that the time has not yet come.

The cost of patents may be amortized over their useful life like plant machinery may be depreciated.

metaphor, mixed. In "the hero is a lion," "lion" is a metaphor for "hero." So is "long arm" for "law" in "the long arm of the law." One creates a little picture of the idea "hero," the other of "law." Run together, however, they yield a picture difficult to visualize: "The hero is a lion who stretches out the long arm of the law." This lion begins to look like an ape. When two or more visually incompatible metaphors such as these run together, the result is a mixed metaphor. In verse we accept mixed metaphors with tolerance; but Hamlet's famous infinitive, "To take up arms against a sea of troubles," would suggest, if it occurred in expository prose, a kind of marine eggbeater. In "Politics and the English Language," George Orwell cites a ludicrous example,

The Fascist octopus has sung its swan song, the jackboot is thrown into the melting pot.

and he comments: "it can be taken for certain that the writer is not seeing a mental image of the objects he is naming; in other words, he is not really thinking." His comment applies just as precisely to a famous mixed metaphor of examination-book origin:

Dante stood with one foot in the Middle Ages, and with the other saluted the rising sun of the Renaissance.

Metaphors in themselves can be effective. You can keep them from turning into ludicrous mixed metaphors by using only one metaphor at a time and making sure that the rest of your sentence is consistent with it:

Achilles is a lion at whose roar both Greeks and Trojans cower.

Safer still, keep as short as possible all sentences containing metaphors, as Emerson does in

The sky is the daily bread of the eyes.

modifier, misplaced. One example should suffice for this very common fault.

A report has been received that the Kennebunkport harbor has been polluted by the Kennebunkport Harbor Commission.

Committees and commissions do very odd things at times, but it seems quite unlikely that if the Kennebunkport Harbor Commission actually polluted its own harbor, it would be so candid as to admit it by compiling a report. The problem, of course, is that the writer meant "by the Kennebunkport Harbor Commission" to modify "received," not "polluted," and should have made it do so by putting the modifying phrase beside the word modified. Always keep modifier and the word modified together to avoid confusion and perhaps bathos.

A report has been received by the Kennebunkport Harbor Commission that Kennebunkport harbor has been polluted.

Now the writer can set to work getting rid of the passive voice in this sentence.

organization arbitrary, lacks logic. See Chapter Four, especially *the outline as route-marking,* pp. 48–50.

overwriting: too many modifiers. See *adjective prostration* and *overwriting,* pp. 113–16.

organization, principle of over-all. See *finding an argument or focus,* pp. 41–43, *a more flexible technique for disposition,* pp. 46–48, especially pp. 46, and *the outline as route-marking,* pp. 48–50.

paragraphing, arbitrary meaningless. See *the visual heresy,* pp. 64–66, *the transfer from outline to paragraph,* pp. 67–68, and *the topic sentence,* pp. 68–71.

paragraphs not developed around single points. See *the transfer from outline to paragraph,* p. 67, and *the topic sentence,* pp. 68–71.

paragraphs, too many short, undeveloped. See *the visual heresy,* pp. 64–66.

paragraph, unnecessary introductory. See Chapter Six, especially *introduction as statement,* pp. 78–79.

parallelism, faulty. Elements in parallel positions in a sentence should have parallel form. Thus, not

Shakespeare's main interests were to write popular plays, to make money, and that he could invest in the players' company

but

Shakespeare's main interests were to write popular plays, to make money, and to invest in the players' company.

Not

Because Shakespeare came from a country town and with only a grammar-school education, he had little experience of the theatre

but

Because Shakespeare came from a country town and had only a grammar-school education, he had little experience of the theatre.

That is, infinitives parallel infinitives, phrases phrases, clauses clauses, nouns nouns, etc.

participle, dangling. This usually occurs when the writer begins a sentence with a participle ("lying," "leaving") intended to modify the subject of the main clause, then changes the subject.

Lying prone through the count of ten, it was clear that Cassius Clay had won another.

Who is lying prone? Apparently not Clay if he is the victor. Here "lying" was meant to modify Clay's opponent, but somewhere in writing the sentence the author lost sight of that opponent, so that "lying" (which should act like an adjective) has nothing to modify. To correct, the writer can either find a noun for the participle to modify or turn "lying prone through the count of ten" into a subordinate clause.

Lying prone through the count of ten, the challenger had obviously lost the fight and Cassius Clay had won another.

When the challenger lay prone through the count of ten, it was clear that Cassius Clay had won another.

This error is best detected by reading aloud. When you begin a sentence with a participle construction, ask yourself if the participle has something to modify.

pronoun should agree with antecedent. In correct writing, a pronoun will agree with the noun it refers back to (the antecedent). "Each," "either," "neither," "everybody," "everyone," "nobody," "person" are correctly singular, so singular pronouns refer back to them.

As for the Army and Navy space programs, each is out for *itself*. (not *themselves*)
Neither Moscow nor Washington employed more than a little of *its* influence in the Congo. (not *their*)
One must decide on *his* own course of study.

In the first two examples above, the plural pronoun is almost universal in American speech but would be considered wrong in most writing.
Collective nouns are considered singular or plural, depending on whether each is thought of as a unit or as a number of individuals:

The crowd maneuvered *itself* slowly against the thin wall of soldiers and police.
The crowd began to bring out Molotov cocktails and other home-made explosives from *their* jackets and sacks.

purple patches. This is a traditional nickname for any bit of unnecessarily ornate writing, sometimes also described by the sarcastic term "fine writing," or when it is long, "purple passage." When I was a senior I wrote for the college magazine an article on the Canadian novel. It was an ordinary, straightforward article, but toward the end, in a discussion of the unwritten "Great Canadian Novel," I waxed eloquent:

We cannot expect the Great Canadian Novel to spring up unaided in our present cultural climate, *like some mystic flower bursting into bloom in the unfertilized desert.*

The baroque flourish (italicized here) is not only unnecessary (it adds nothing to the idea of the sentence) but distracting: it draws attention to itself as a calculated device and thereby to the writer's self-conscious artiness. Purple patches tend to occur toward the close of the paper as part of the attempt to end with a bang. Watch out for them if you find yourself laboring to think up an unusual bit of imagery or metaphor purely for the purposes of ornament. See also *metaphors*, above, *elegant variation*, p. 118, and *if you like it, cross it out*, p. 135.

questions, rhetorical. One of the most common undergraduate mannerisms, the rhetorical question is really a statement in question form:

What is chalk? It is little more than carbonic acid and quicklime.
What family of plants contains the most species? The answer, surprisingly, is the orchid family.

The reader sees that these questions were asked only because the author knew the answers, and so the effect rings false. Use the device sparingly and then only to draw attention to an important crux in your material. Never use it in an attempt to jazz up ordinary pedestrian facts. The best question is the question to which no one answer is surely known:

Is there some historical fact concealed behind the myth of the lost continent of Atlantis?
Exactly what are flying saucers?

But these are true, not rhetorical, questions.

quotation marks, apologetic. See *apologetic quotation marks,* p. 127.

quotation marks, comma comes inside. It is a rule of American punctuation (though not of British) that when a comma or a period coincides with the second of a set of quotation marks, it always comes inside the quotation mark.

"You are wrong, sir," he said.
He said, "You are wrong, sir."
The technique, called "meiosis," is. . . .
The technique is called "meiosis."

But *colon* and *semicolon* always come outside the second quotation mark.

The judge referred to the "quality of mercy":. . . .
First, the judge referred to the "quality of mercy"; then. . . .

Question mark and *exclamation mark* come inside if part of the quotation, outside if they are not.

"Have you any nickels?" he asked.
When did you read Mann's "Death in Venice"?

"Everyone on stage!" shouted the director.

How could I have forgotten the author of "The Short Happy Life of Francis Macomber"!

quotations dovetailed into text. When you quote, make sure that you phrase the introduction to your quotation so that it fits the quotation grammatically. The introduction and the quotation together then become grammatically a single sentence. Here are two lines from *Macbeth* inaccurately introduced:

Sick at heart and despairing, Macbeth thinks of time only as "Tomorrow and tomorrow and tomorrow/Creep in this petty pace from day to day."

The whole sentence works until "Creep," where it becomes clear that the quotation, a complete sentence in its own right, has been made object of the preposition "as." "Creeping" would solve the problem but commit a worse sin by making the quotation inaccurate. So the introduction must be arranged to make the quotation a subordinate clause within the larger sentence:

Sick at heart and despairing, Macbeth sees in time only that "Tomorrow and tomorrow and tomorrow/Creep in this petty pace from day to day."

semicolon misused (confused with colon). Few undergraduates discriminate between colon and semicolon. The *colon* is best understood as (1) an equals sign, used as in algebra to denote an equation:

He made out his grocery list: pickles, mustard, ketchup, relish, and cokes.

Here the colon points out that the "pickles" series equals the "grocery list." It also introduces quotations, as it does the grocery-list quotation above. In this case, the idea of equation is prominent: the introductory sentence tells what the equation will illustrate, then comes a colon, then the equation illustrates. (2) The colon can also anticipate result:

He ran his fingers over the little keyboard: there was an odd pause, then a startling clash of bells from the southwest tower.

The colon is strong punctuation and thus should never interrupt the grammatical structure of the sentence. It should come only when a clause is complete.

A new shooter will make the errors of: flinching, jerking, bucking, and closing his eyes.

To jam a colon between a preposition and its subject is to ignore and thus violate the grammar of the sentence. The colon should occur only if it is preceded by a word that sums up the second half of the equation ("the following" will do if there is nothing else).

A new shooter will make the following errors: flinching, jerking, bucking, and closing his eyes.

When you can say to yourself "the following" or "the result" at the point where you want the colon, then it is accurate punctuation.

The *semicolon* is very different. It is really a powerful comma and invaluable in situations where a comma would be weak or confusing. It is useful (1) to separate the main clauses of a compound sentence (which may contain commas in themselves):

A new shooter will make many errors, some of them unavoidable; but his worst mistake will be failure to take note of his errors in his scorebook.

(2) to keep together two or three closely related independent clauses:

A new shooter will make many errors, some of them unavoidable; his worst mistake, however, will be failure to take note of his errors in his scorebook.

(3) to avoid confusion when elements in a series contain commas:

A new shooter will make many errors: flinching, a reaction caused by fear of the recoil; jerking, or pulling the trigger with the whole forearm; bucking, or anticipating the recoil; closing his eyes, which is a kind of flinch; and, worst of all, failing to take note of his errors in his scorebook.

If it were not for the semicolons in the last sentence, we would be unable to distinguish the separate shooting errors from the elements modifying them. Note also the use of the colon here. If you remember that the colon is an equals sign and the semicolon is a super-comma, you will never mistake one for the other.

sentence fragment. The minimum requirement for a sentence is one independent clause with its own subject and verb. Anything less is known as a "sentence fragment." The fragment is commonly the result of an afterthought.

Then we came to the cathedral of Chartres. One of the most famous medieval buildings.

The day closed cold and threatening. Sometimes with gusts of wind.

The Braves made two runs in the ninth. Thus tying the score.

In each case the sentence has been closed with a period, then a detail has been added. This may excusably occur in a first draft, but the writer should see the error when he revises. If he reads the draft aloud, he cannot miss it, even if he knows no grammar. Occasionally, of course, it may be effective to have a partial sentence stand by itself for emphasis or exclamation:

Suddenly far-off thunder and a freshening wind!

Use this device only when you can tell yourself why you want it.

sentences, logical connection between. See *connective and transitional signposts*, pp. 71–73.

sentence to sentence, logical sequence of thought from. See *connective and transitional signposts*, pp. 71–73.

sentence, run-on. Sometimes called run-together sentence or comma-splice, the run-on occurs when two complete sentences have been written as one, usually separated only by a comma.

The Democrats have always controlled the South, the Republicans are now attempting to gain some power, however.

The Stalinist brand of communism demands complete acquiescence from the citizen, it is in some ways a secular religion.

In revision, the writers should have heard that in each case, two complete sentences are punctuated as if they were one. Reading out loud will usually catch the discrepancy. The solution is to punctuate as two separate sentences or to join them with a semicolon or to subordinate one to the other.

The Stalinist brand of communism demands complete acquiescence from the citizen. It is in some ways a secular religion.

The Stalinist brand of communism demands complete acquiescence from the citizen; it is in some ways a secular religion.

Because the Stalinist brand of communism demands complete acquiescence from the citizen, it is in some ways a secular religion.

Sometimes you may want to keep short, relative sentences together in one sentence to get an effect of accumulation:

He put in his thumb, he pulled out a plum, he said, "What a good boy am I!"

Cortez had taken Mexico, Pizarro had climbed to the city of the Inca, DeSoto and Coronado had trekked through the Southwest.

Use this device only when you can tell yourself why you want it.

sentences too interrupted: keep subject and verb together. As a general rule it is wise to keep subject and verb together. Because they are the core of the sentence, it loses impact when words interrupt subject and verb unnecessarily.

The blues, one of the most original products of southern Negro culture, are attracting a new audience by their deep simplicity and emotional honesty.

One of the most original products of southern Negro culture, the blues are attracting a new audience by their deep simplicity and emotional honesty.

Basil Richards cultivated the interruption of subject and verb until it became a debilitating mannerism of his style. But there are times when such an interruption will serve you well. See the *suspended sentence*, pp. 102–3.

sentences too long and complicated. See *state first, qualify afterwards*, p. 115, and *how many words?* pp. 118–20.

sentence to sentence, logical sequence of thought from. See *connective and transitional signposts*, pp. 71–73.

split infinitives. There is a traditional sweeping prohibition against split infinitives ("to crushingly retort," "to valiantly die," "to forever break off"). It is true that split infinitives are often clumsy: "to generously give" ("to give generously" is the familiar and natural order), "to clearly think out" (we expect "to think out clearly"), "to hopelessly fail" ("to fail hopelessly" is expected). But it is often clumsier to avoid splitting the infinitive: "to understand really" is ten times worse than "to really understand"; "to alter much" than "to much alter"; "to forbid flatly" than "to flatly forbid." The best policy is to split infinitives only when the alternative forces you into clumsy word order. In any case, never let more than a single adverb split the infinitive: "to at all costs and by every means available determine" is inexcusable.

square brackets for insertions inside quotations. When you must insert an explanation to make clear some reference in a quotation, do so within square brackets to distinguish your addition from the quotation and thus preserve its accuracy for the reader, as in this from Thoreau:

> The birds I heard today, which, fortunately, did not come within the scope of my science [he could not identify them], sang as freshly as if it had been the first morning of creation.

Make such editorial insertions only when essential to the understanding of the quotation, for they inevitably mar it. (If you have no key for brackets on your typewriter, draw them in with a pen.)

style, monotonous: sentences all beginning with subjects. See *the washboard effect*, pp. 96–98.

style, monotonous: sentences all of similar length. See *the sedative effect*, pp. 95–96.

"to whoever has" (not "whomever"). This is a tricky problem. Here is a sentence with a "whoever" noun clause:

> Entrance to the course is open to whoever has the qualifications.

"Whoever" is the subject of the clause and thus cannot be object of the preposition "to"). In the sentence

> She sang South African folk songs to whomever she could interest.

the form is "whomever," again not because of the preposition "to" but because it is object of the verb "could interest" inside its own clause. The same rule applies to "who" and "whom":

determine the form by the function of the word inside its own clause.

transitions. See *connective and transitional signposts,* pp. 71–73.

underlining for emphasis. This is a much too mechanical means of emphasis to be commonly used. A skilled writer arranges the order of words in a sentence to achieve emphasis where he wants it. It is primitive to write:

Everyone *must* demand *everything* he has a *right* to.

(Note that underlining in handwriting or typing will become italics in print.) See also *common sense about emphasis,* pp. 105–7.

verb should agree with nearer subject after "or." This is a fine point of grammar. "Two cats or one dog is. . ." is correct, not "Two cats or one dog are. . . ." Similarly, "One dog or two cats are . . . ," not "One dog or two cats is. . . ."

verb should agree with subject. It is a basic rule of grammar that verbs agree with their subjects. We automatically say "I have," not "I has," and "we think," not "we thinks." The only difficulty occurs when a plural idea separates a singular subject from its verb (or vice versa).

Among the small boats of New England, one of the once numerous types *is* the Gloucester dory. (not *are*)

The tracks of a very large cougar, perhaps the same animal glimpsed yesterday for a moment in the pine scrub, *were* still visible in the snow. (not *was*)

Collective nouns like "people," "jury," and "crowd" create another kind of problem in agreement: are they singular or plural? The answer depends on what you mean by "people," etc. If you mean the people as a unit, then use a singular verb; if you mean people as a collection of individuals, then use a plural verb.

"The people, sir, is a great beast," said Alexander Hamilton.

If the people are hit by another recession, they will use their votes to demolish the government.

verbiage, deadwood. See *how many words?* pp. 118–20, and *cut away the fat*, p. 133.

verbs, passive. See *verbs and impotency*, pp. 111–13.

verb tenses, instability of. In any passage make one verb tense basic and use it consistently as a point of temporal reference. Suppose it is the past tense: if you refer to a point further back in time, use the pluperfect ("had"); if to what is still true, use the present; if to the future, use "would."

Julius Caesar *was* an indefatigable imperialist. In 55 B.C. he *stretched* Roman power to its northwest extreme when he *invaded* Britain. Before that, he *had subdued* Gaul, the country that now *is* France. Later he *would assume* power in Rome herself. But his invasion of Britain *was* no easy fight.

It is conventional to treat time in works of literature as present (sometimes called the "historic present"). When you describe action in literature, then, make the present tense basic, use past for past, and future for future.

When Ishmael *signs up* for the voyage of the Pequod, he *has* no idea that Captain Ahab *is* half mad and once *lost* a leg in an engagement with a mysterious white whale. Much later he *will learn* that Ahab's *pursuit* of that whale *is* a mad, allegorical quest of mythic proportions and that the voyage *will* end in disaster, which only Ishmael himself *will* survive.

word-choice, pretentious. Always use the simplest word that says precisely what you mean. See *choosing a level of diction*, pp. 124–27, noting especially "indoor" and "outdoor" words.

Index